Mandala Coloring Pages

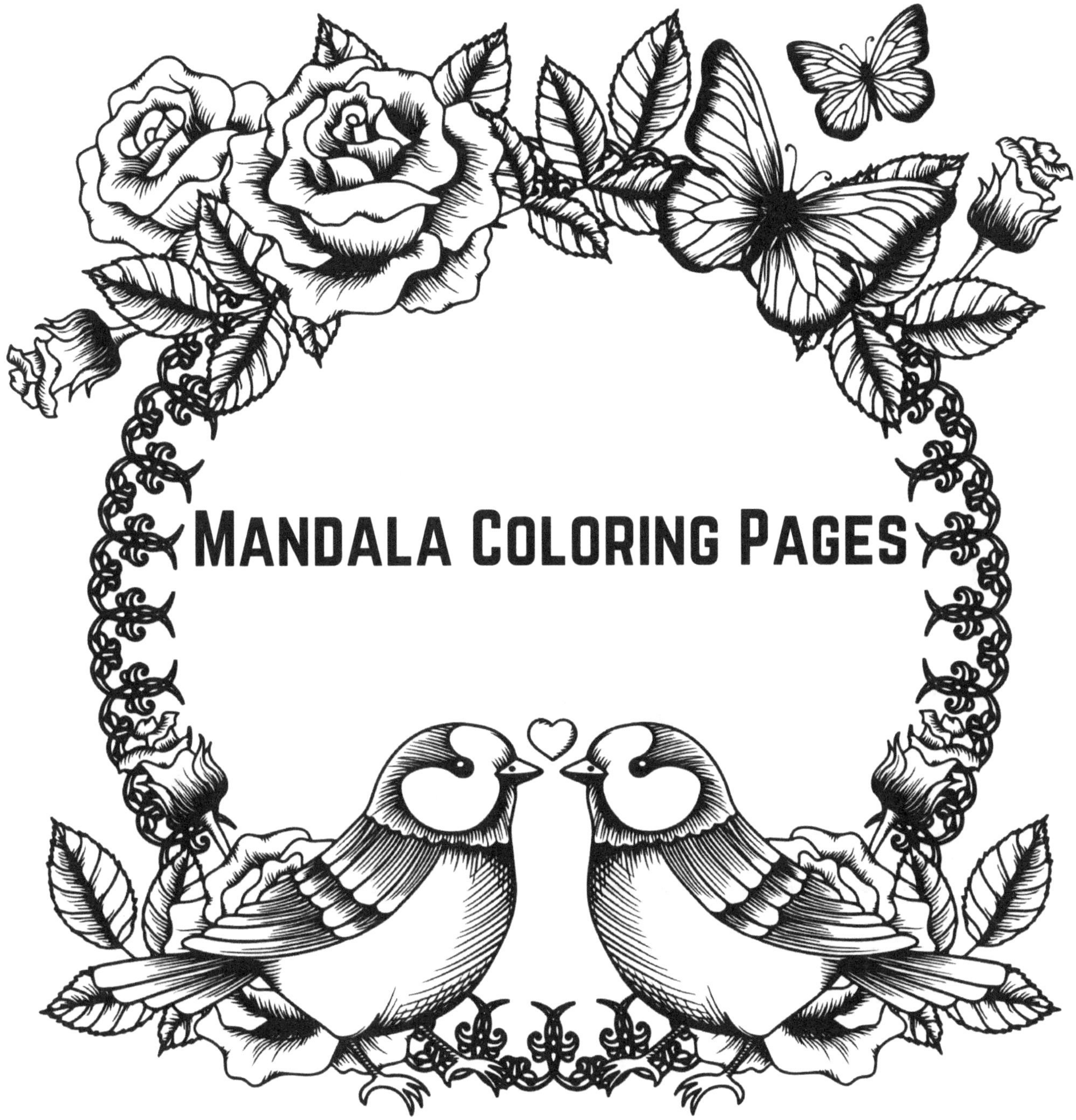

VIP VOLT

All Rights Reserved

This Coloring Book Belongs To :

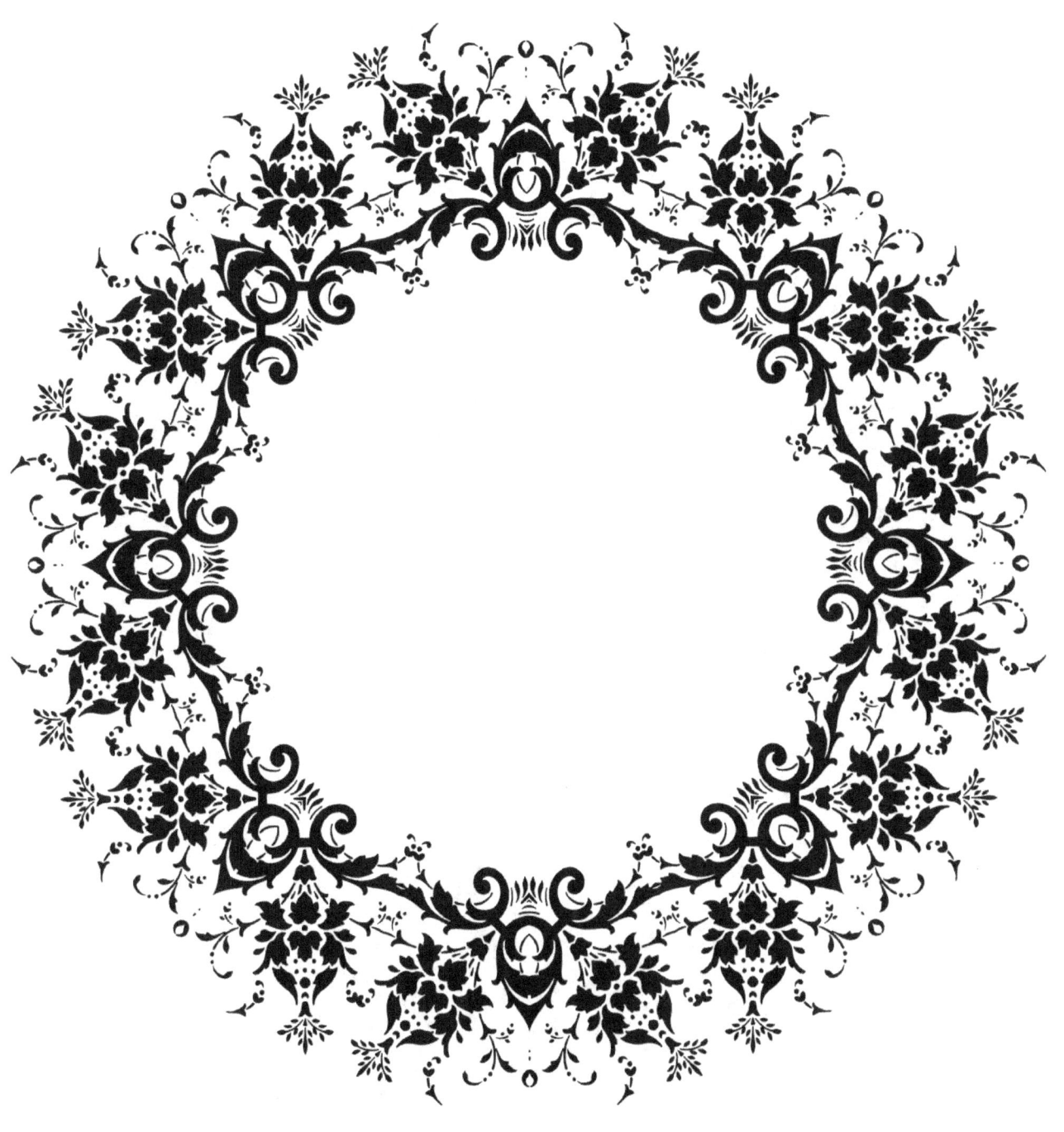

Quick Coloring Tip:

If you use markers, it is a good practice to use thick paper on the back of the page so that the ink does not stain the next page.

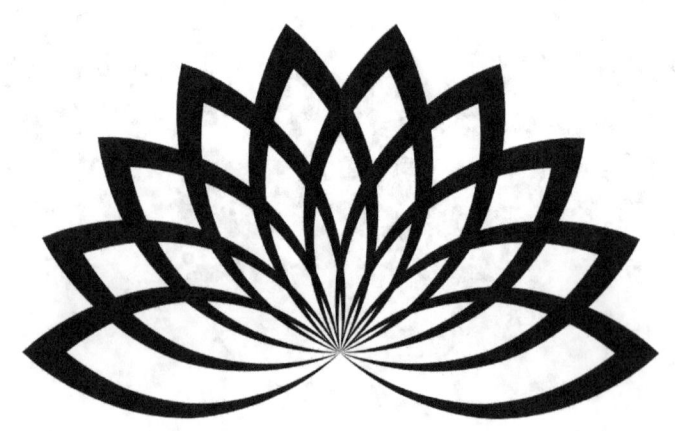

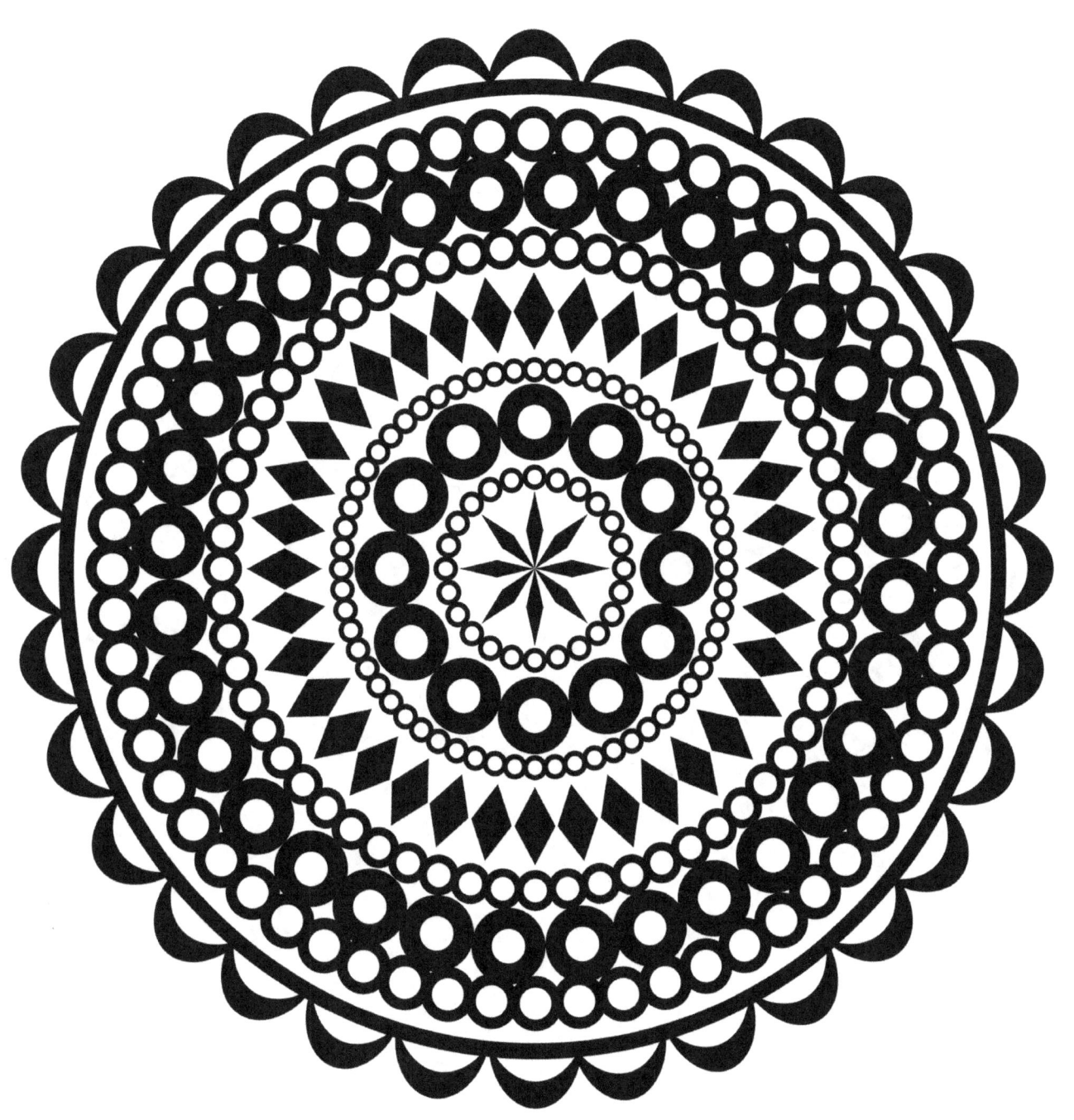

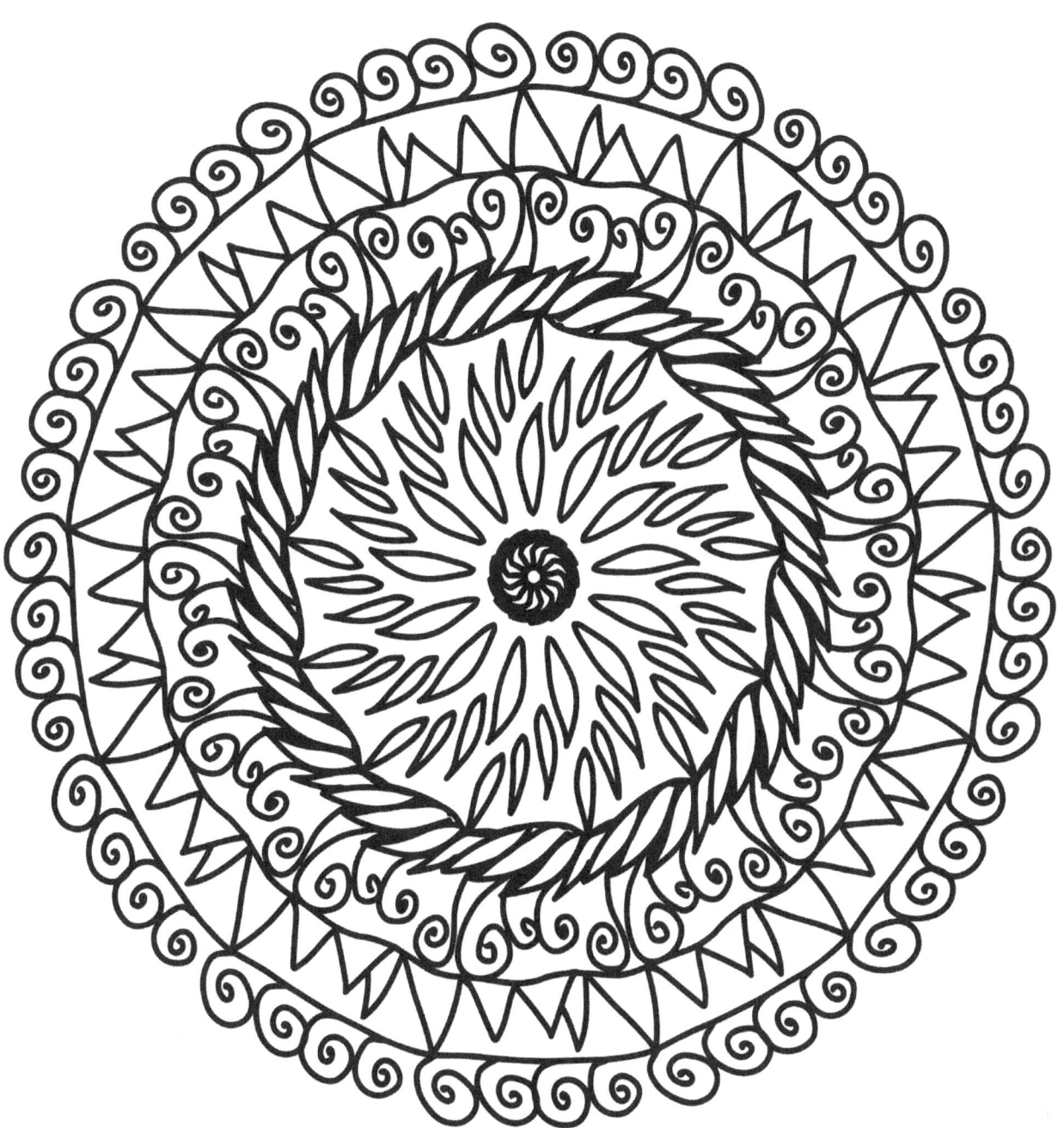

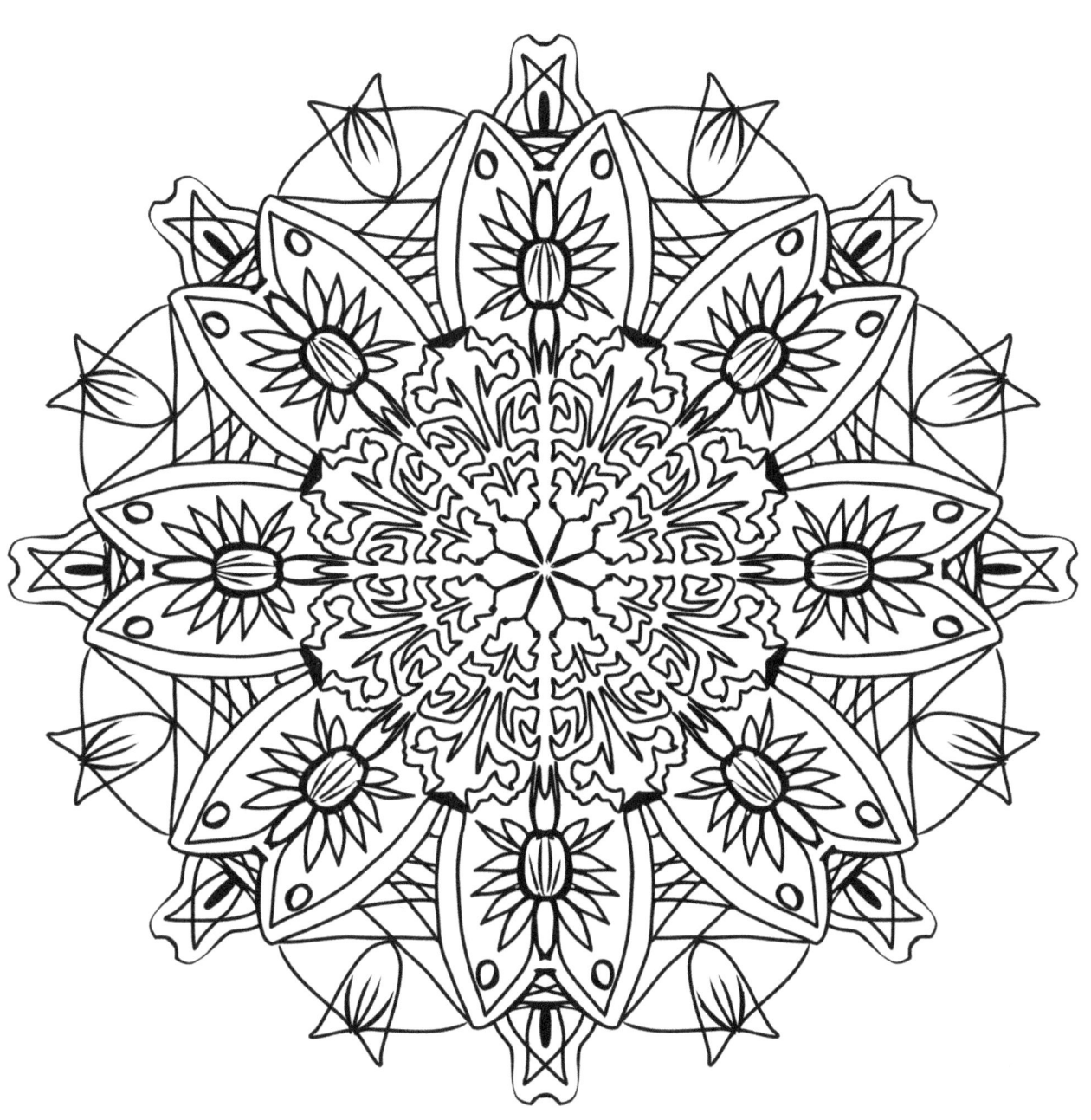

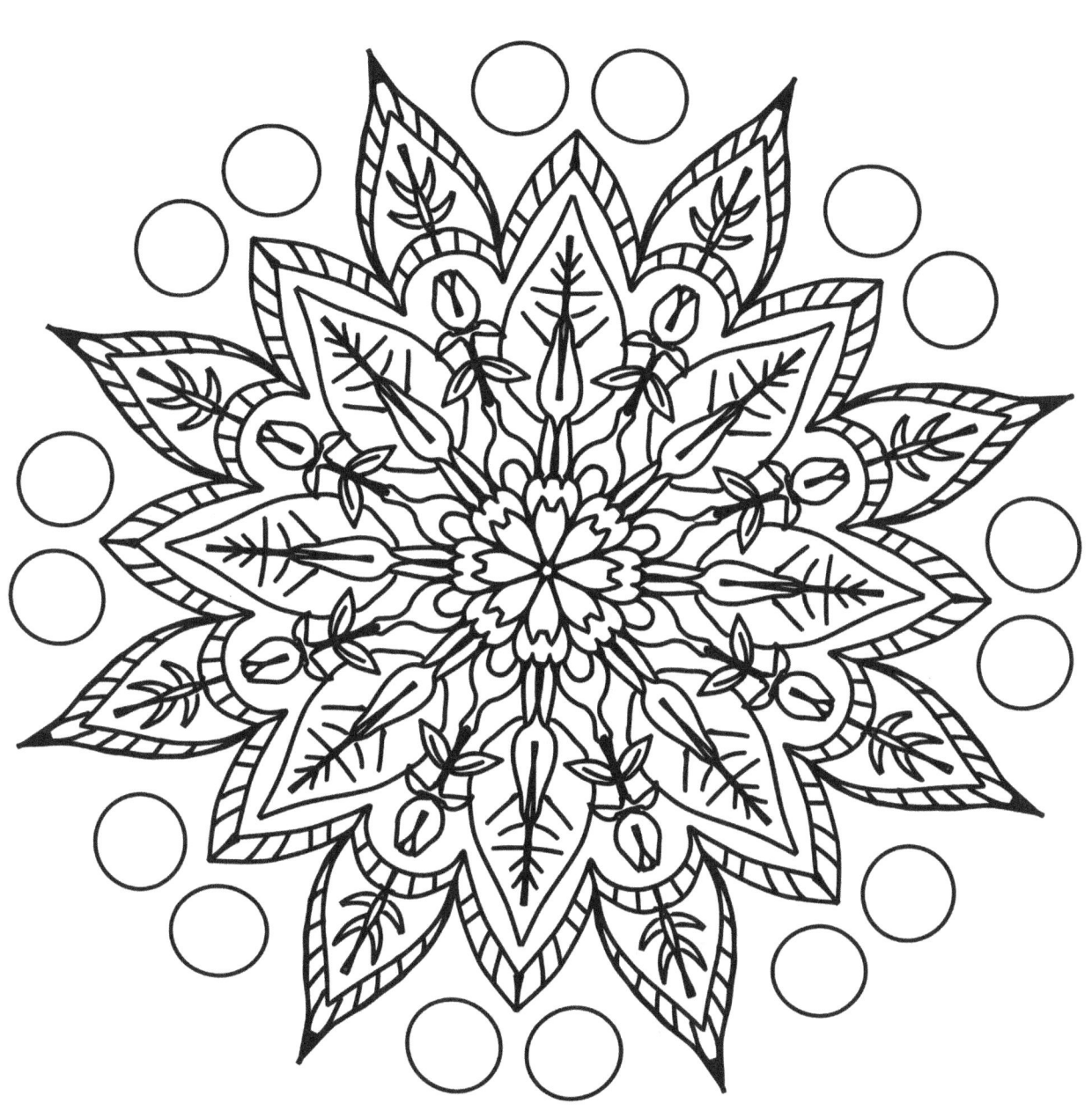

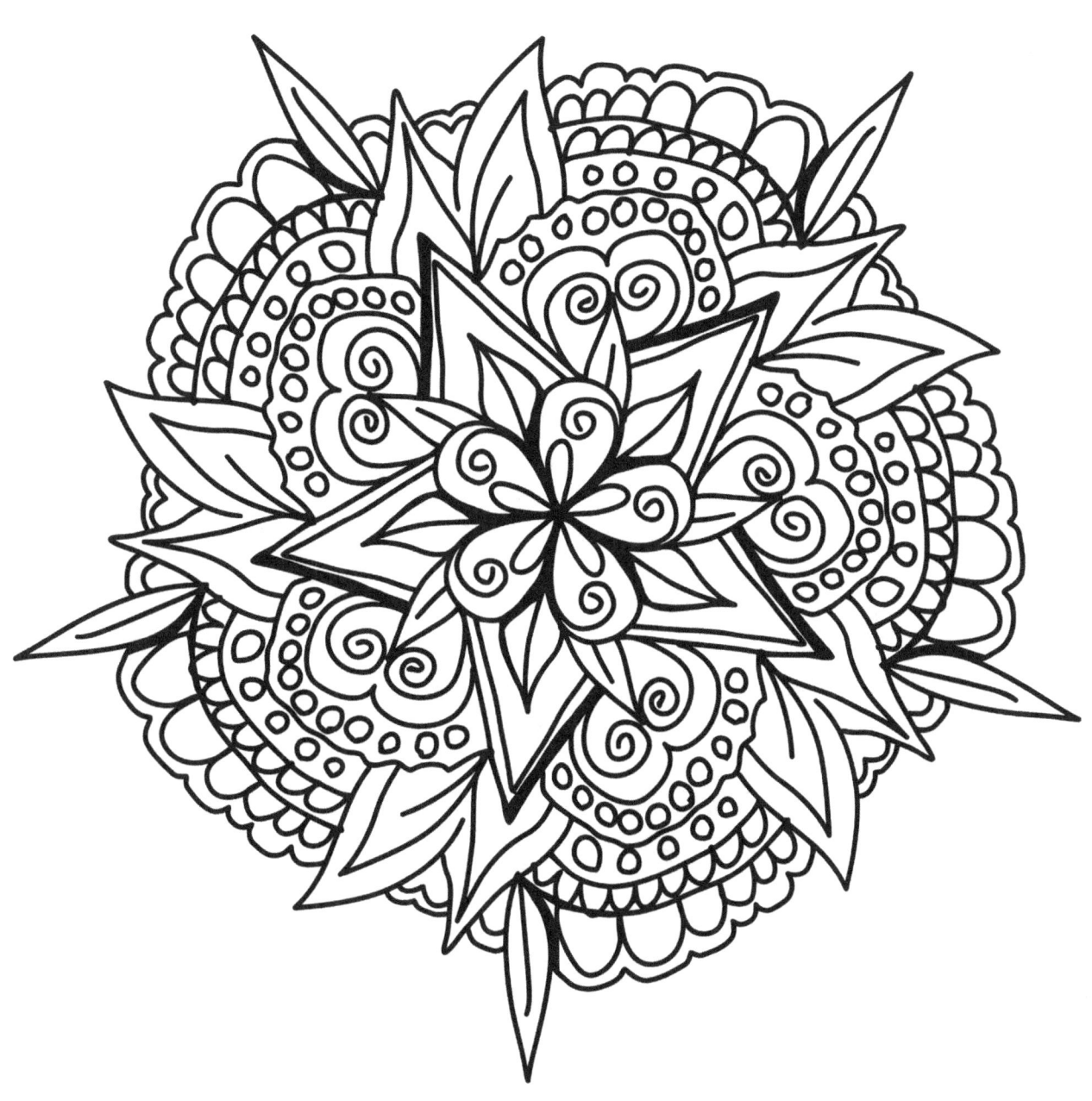

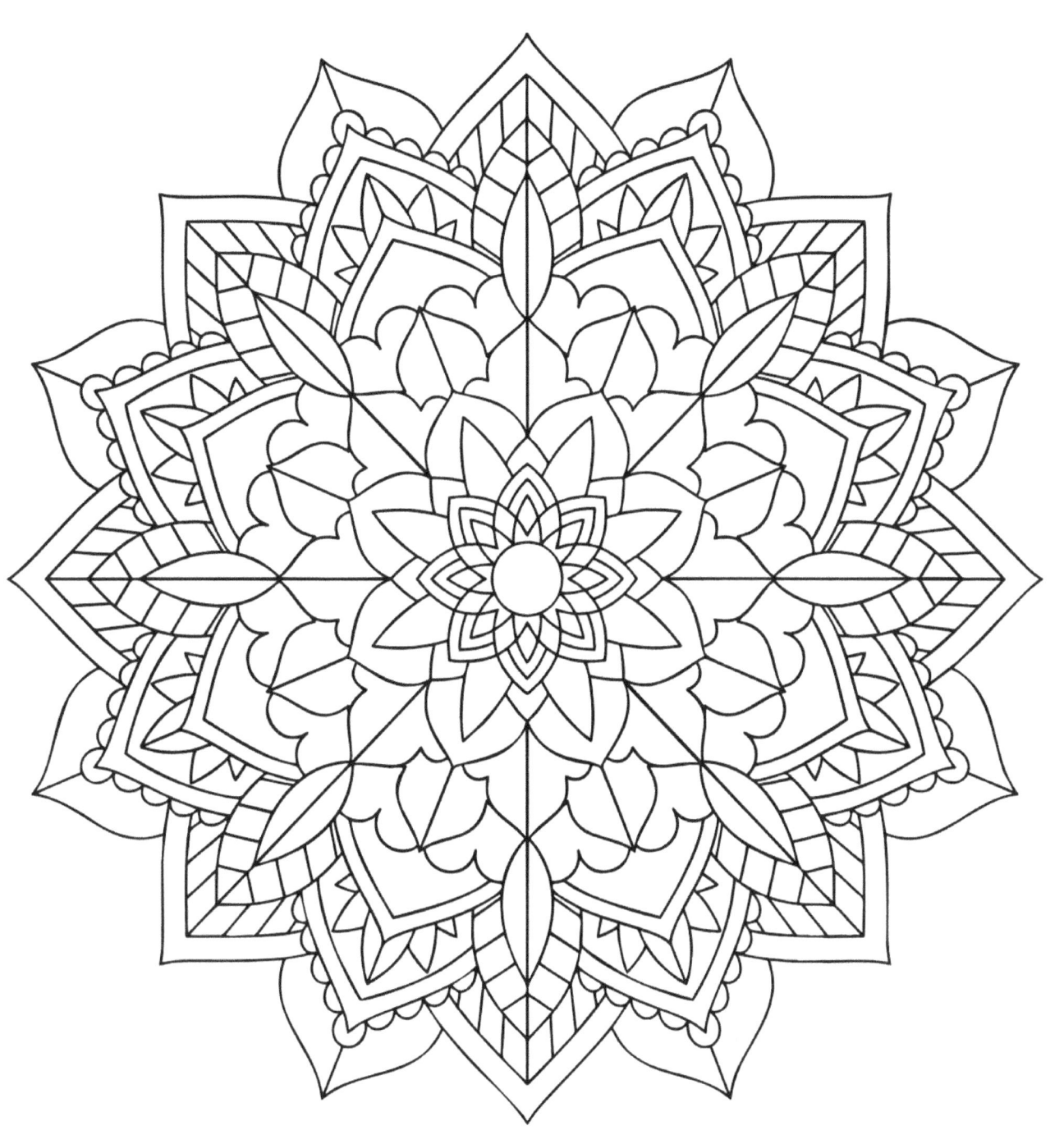

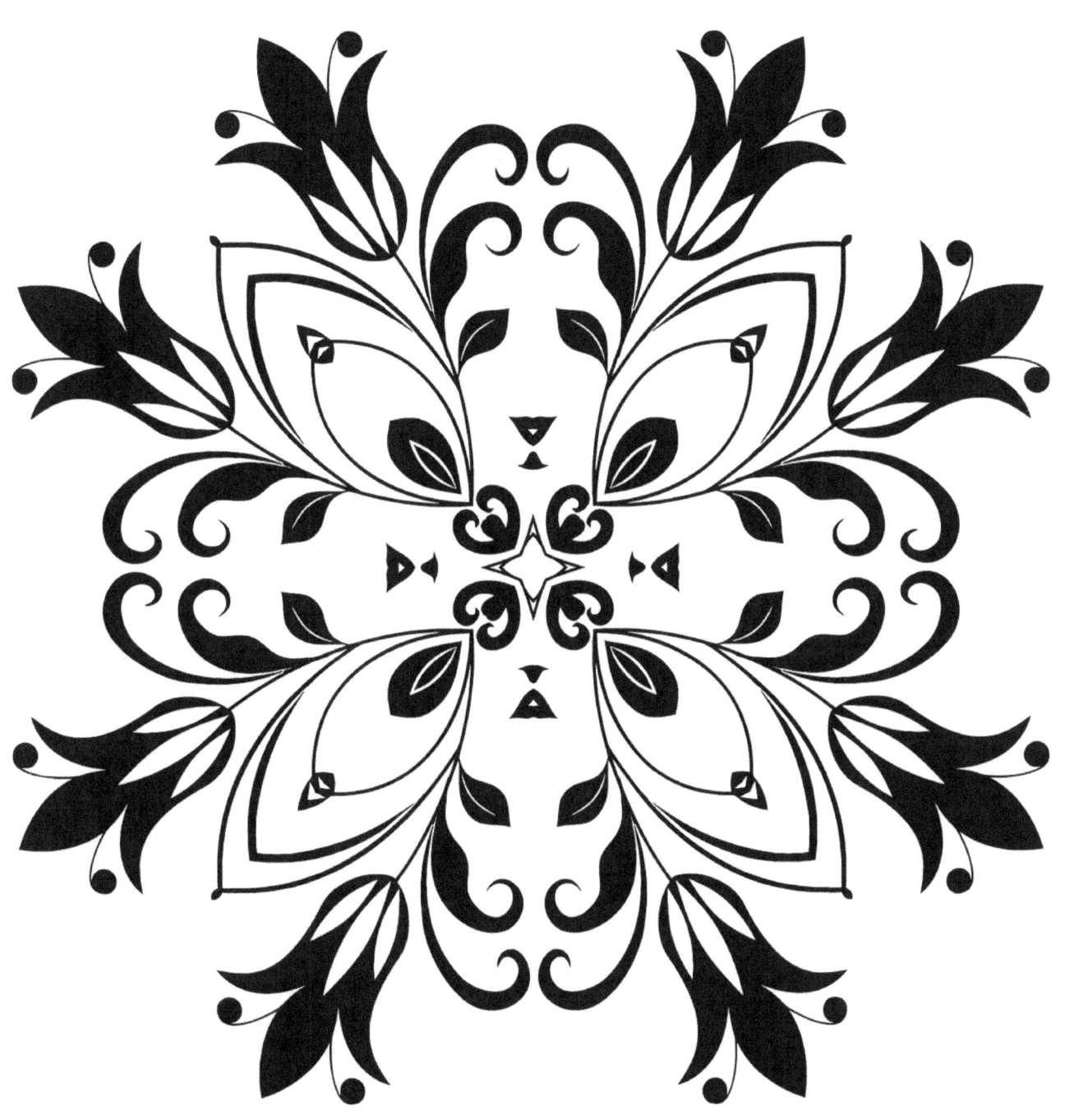

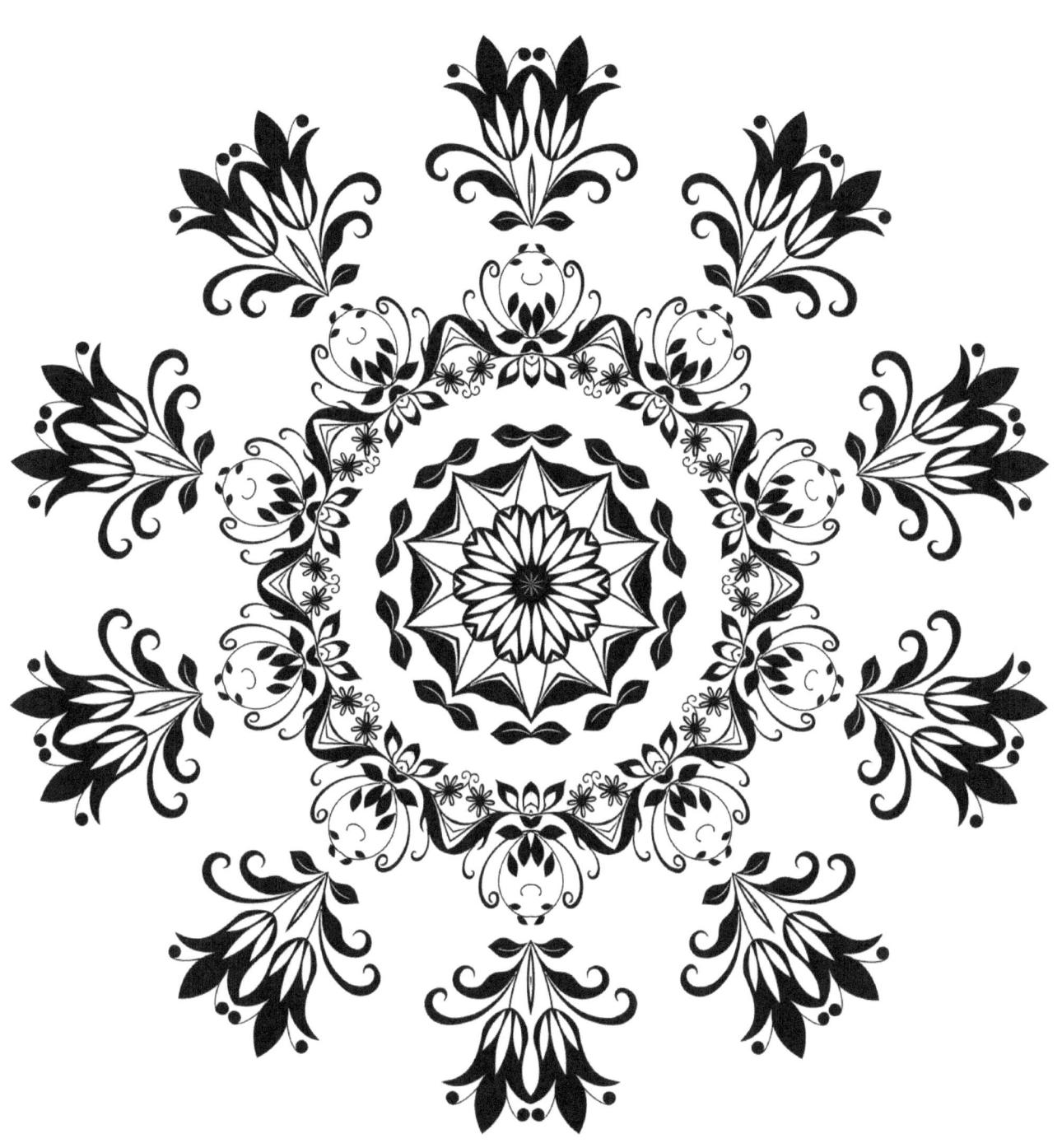

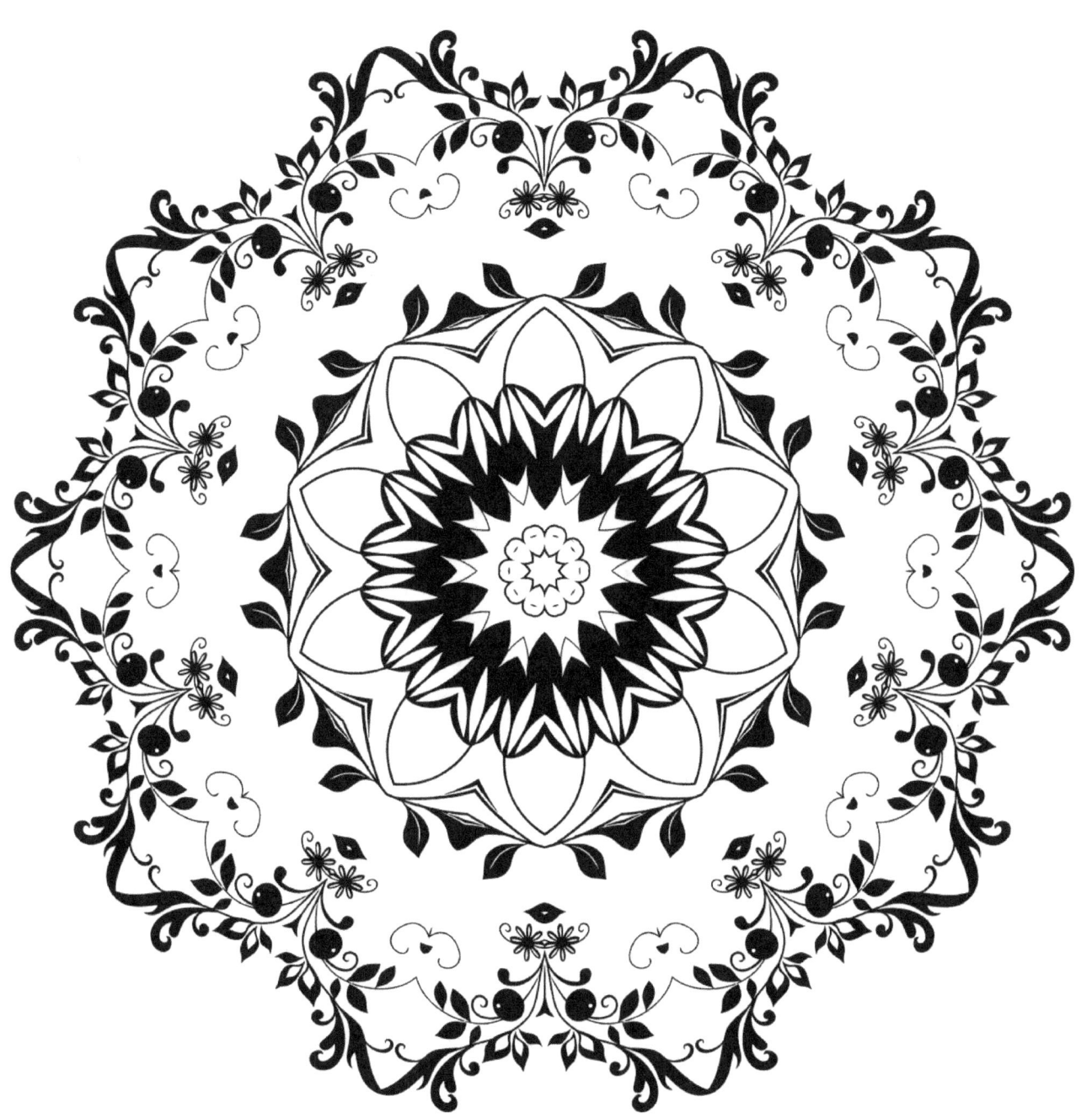

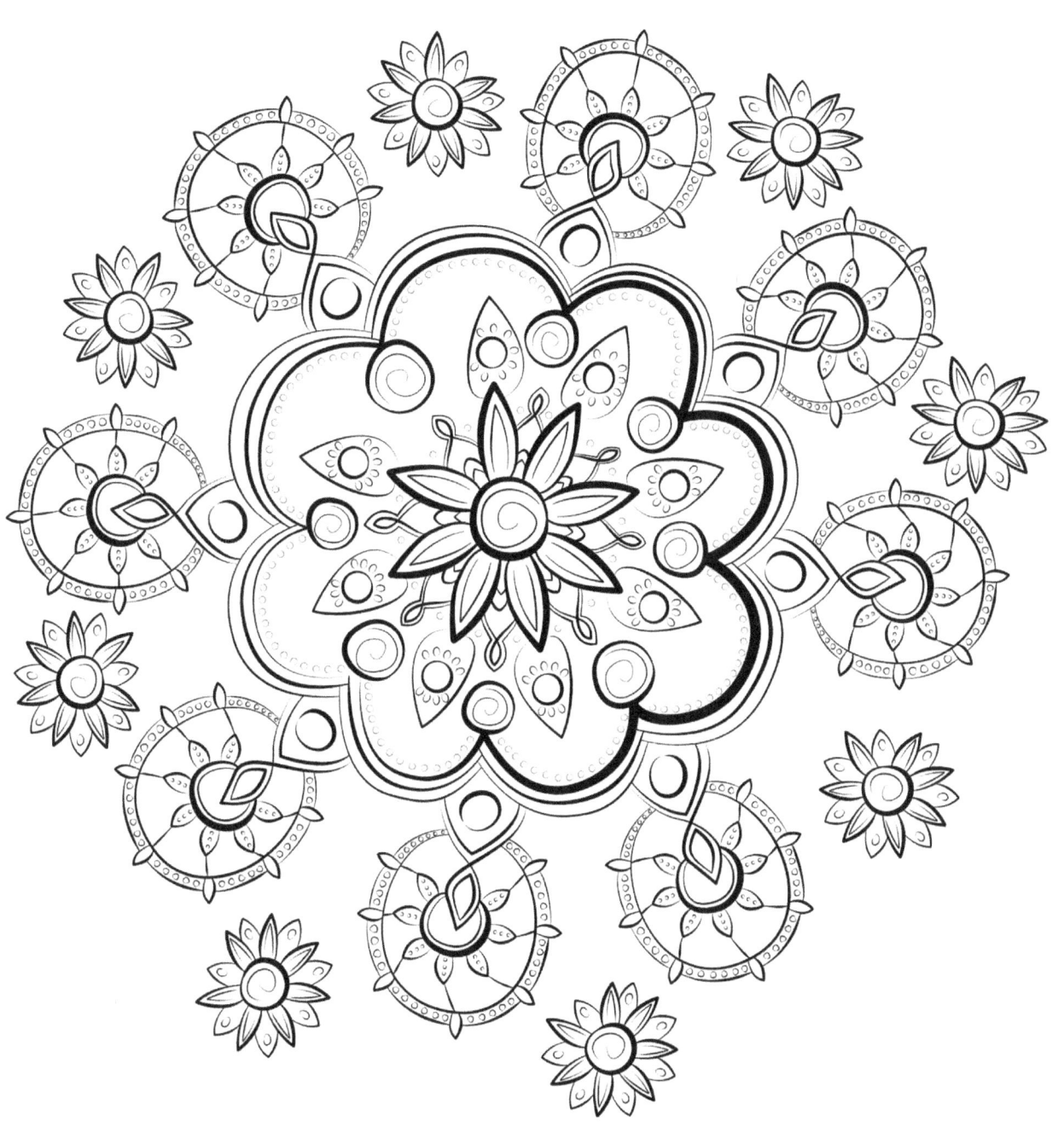

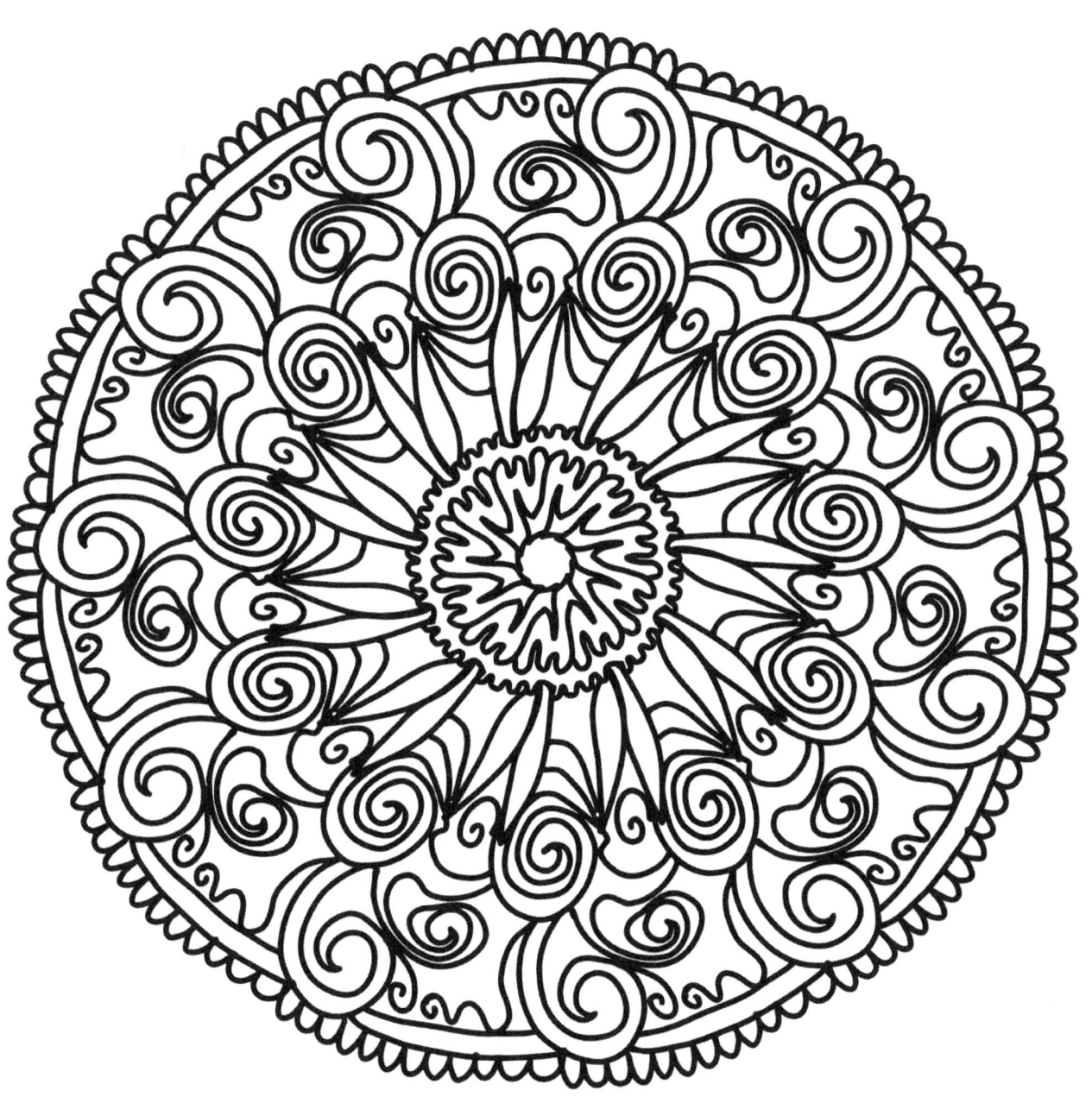

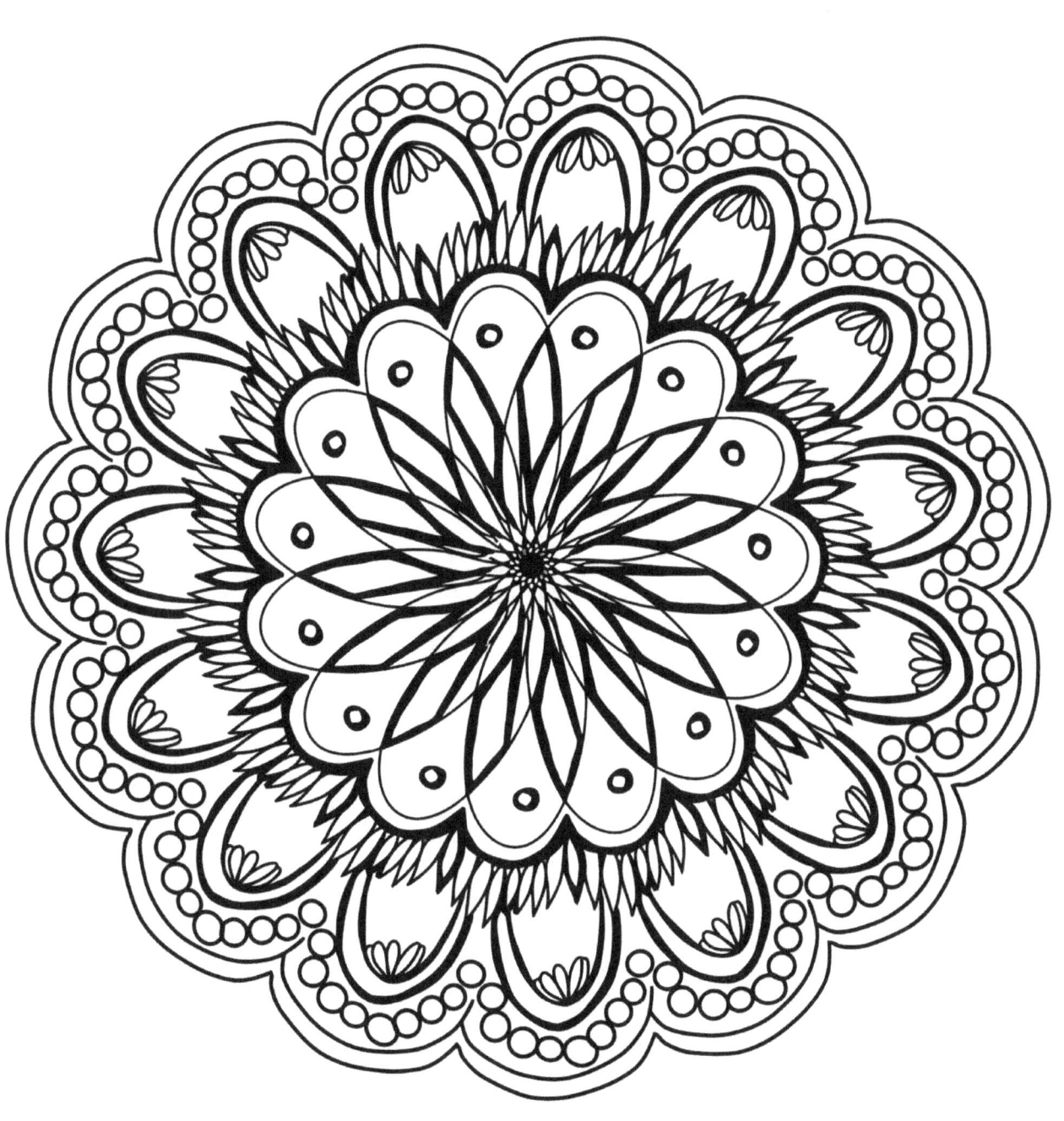

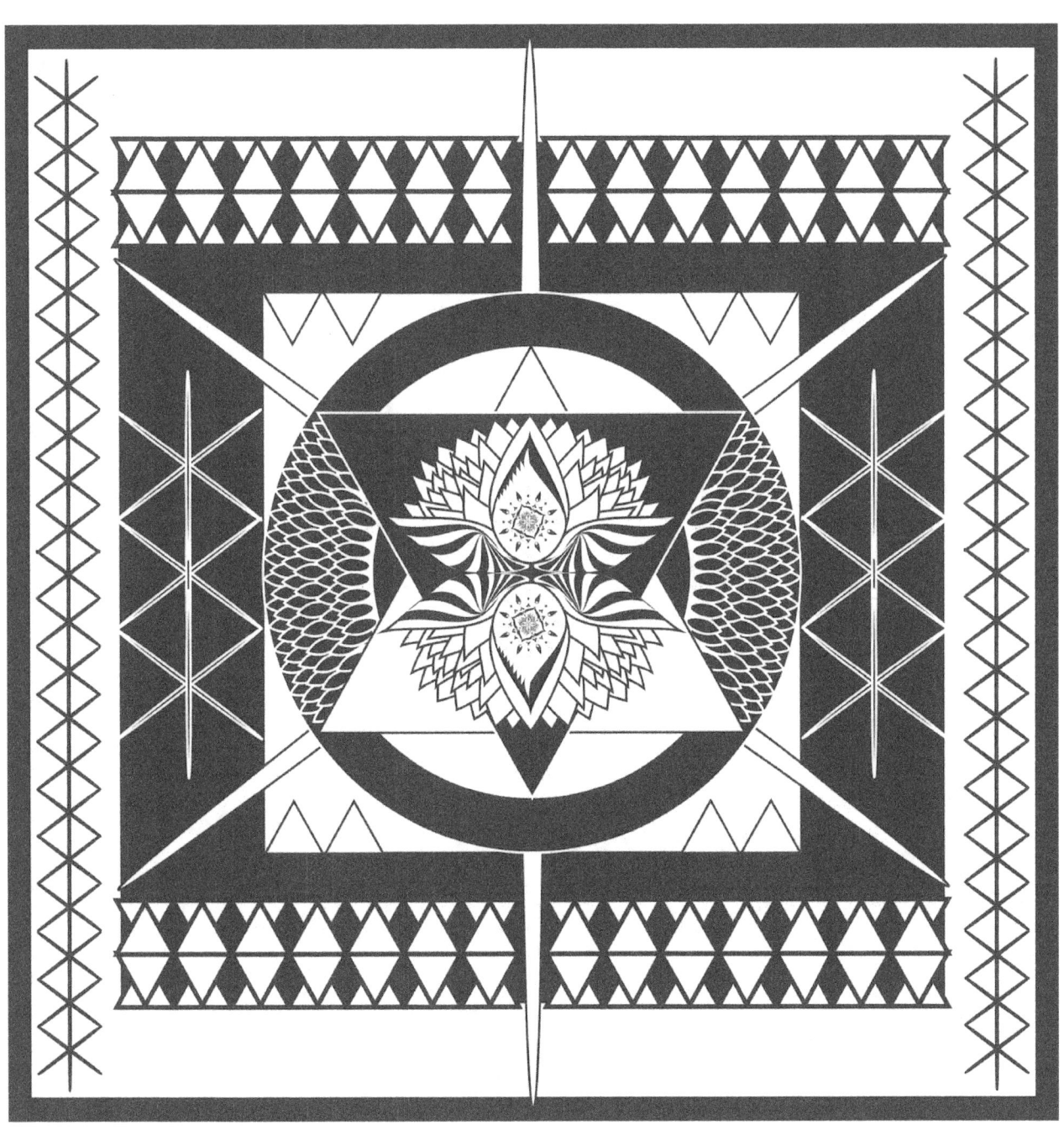

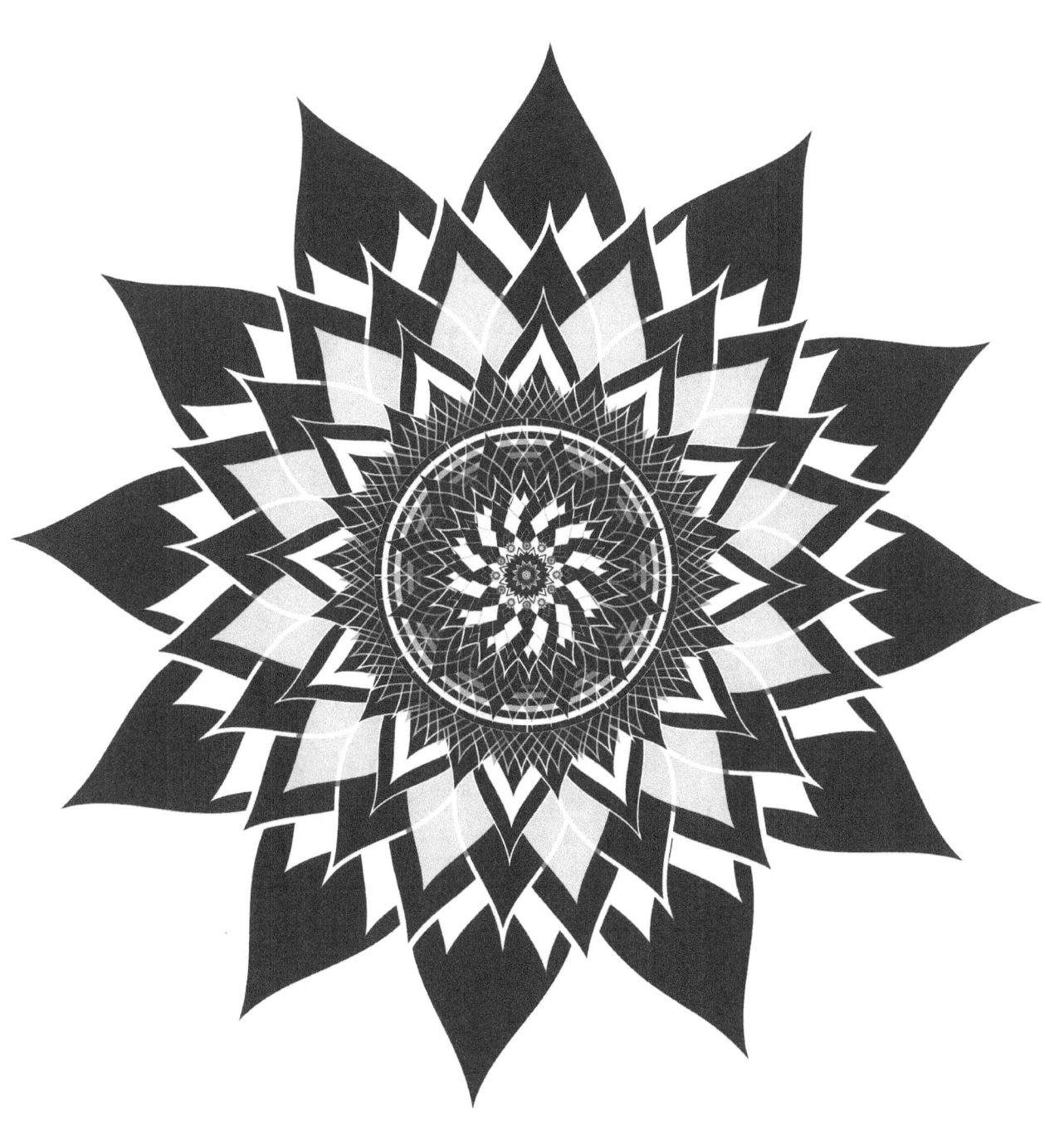

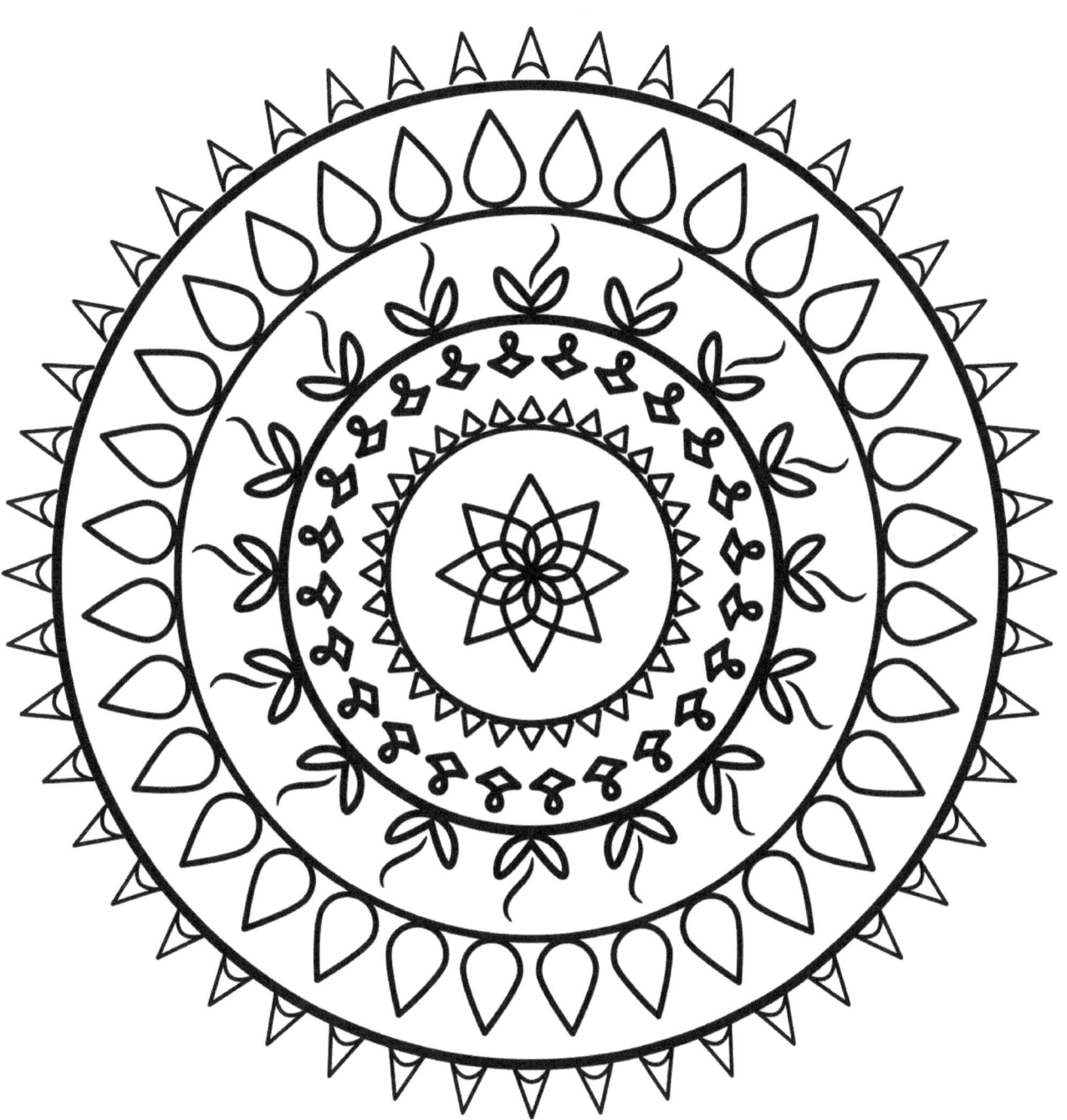

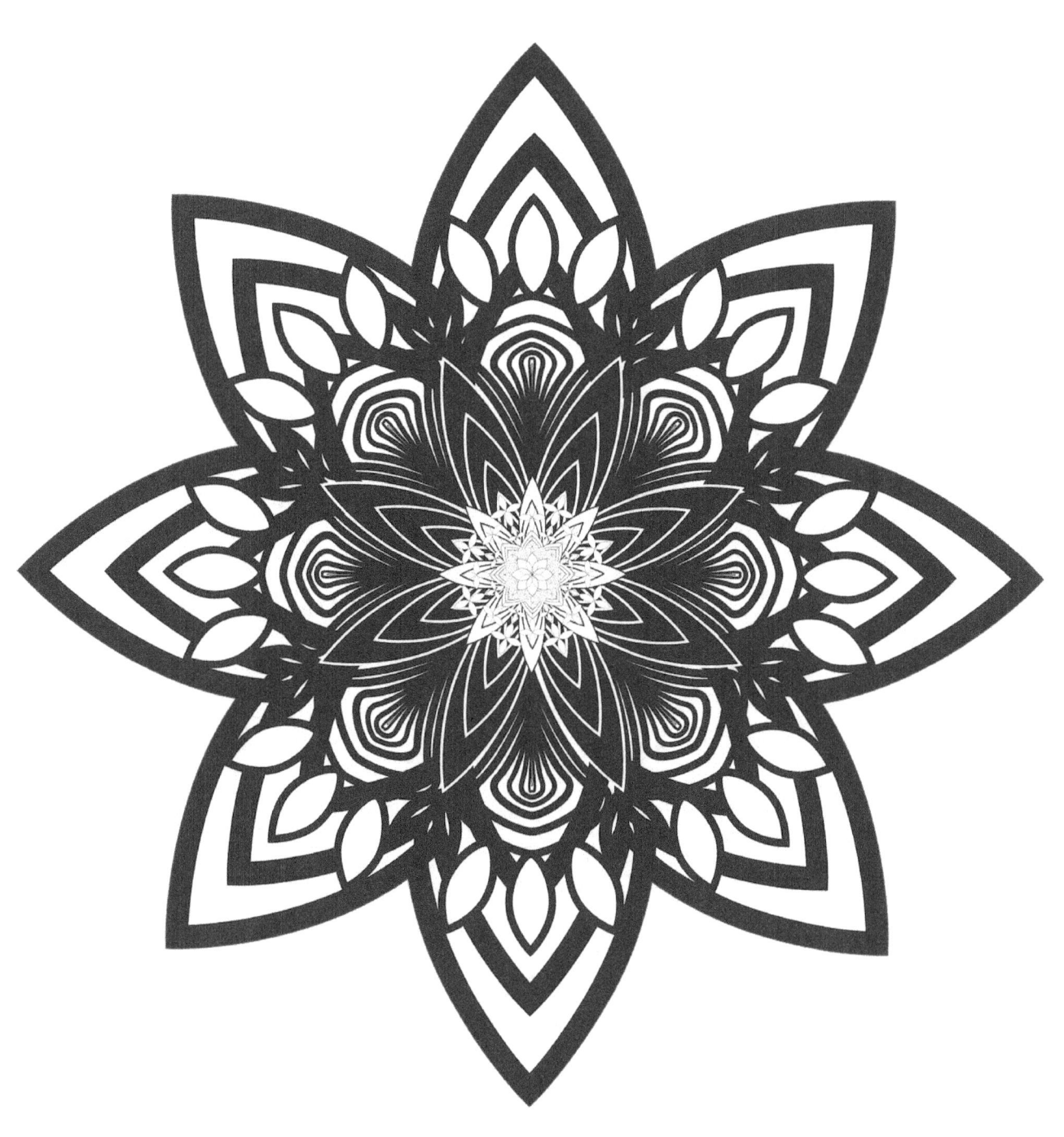

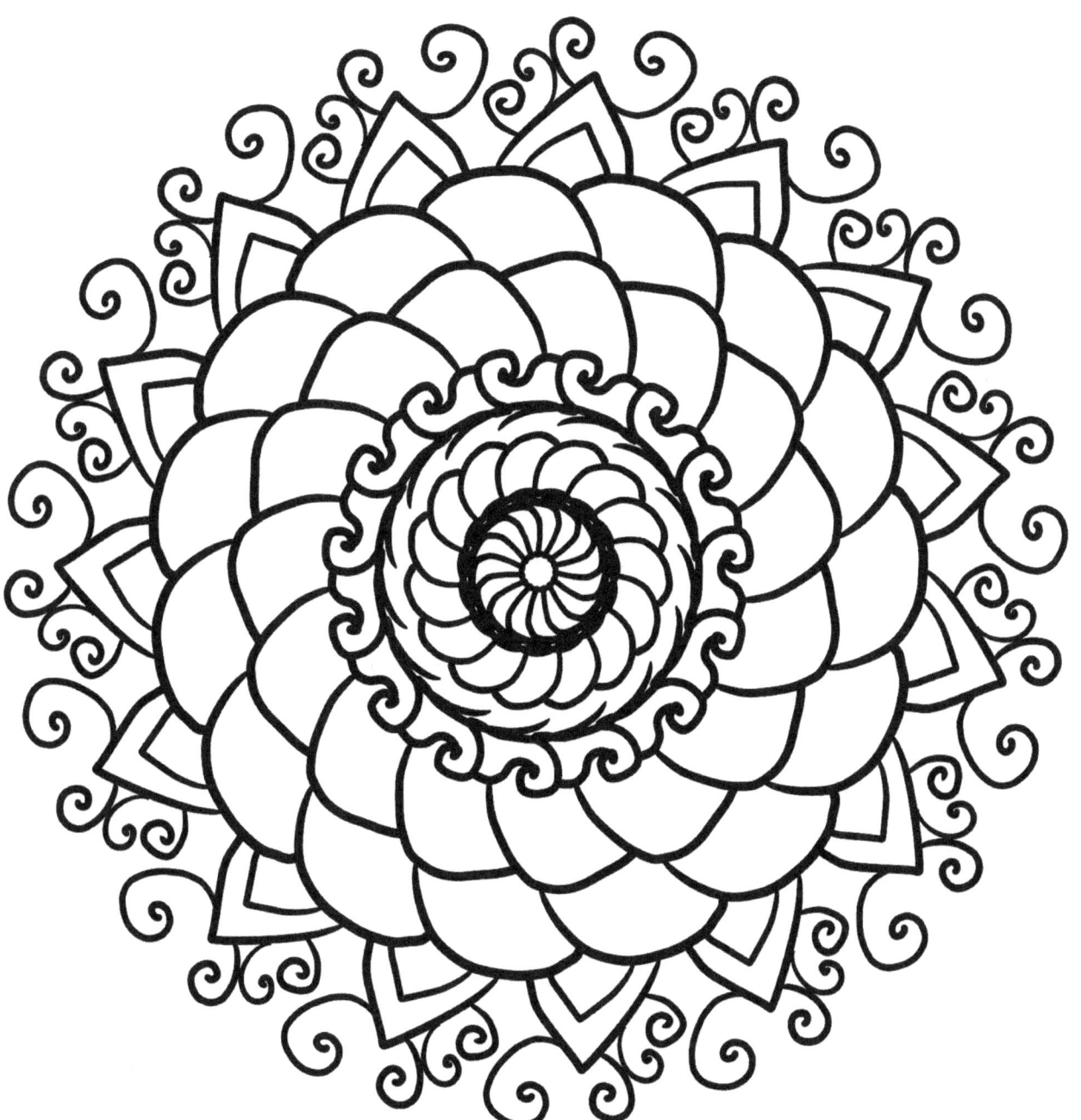

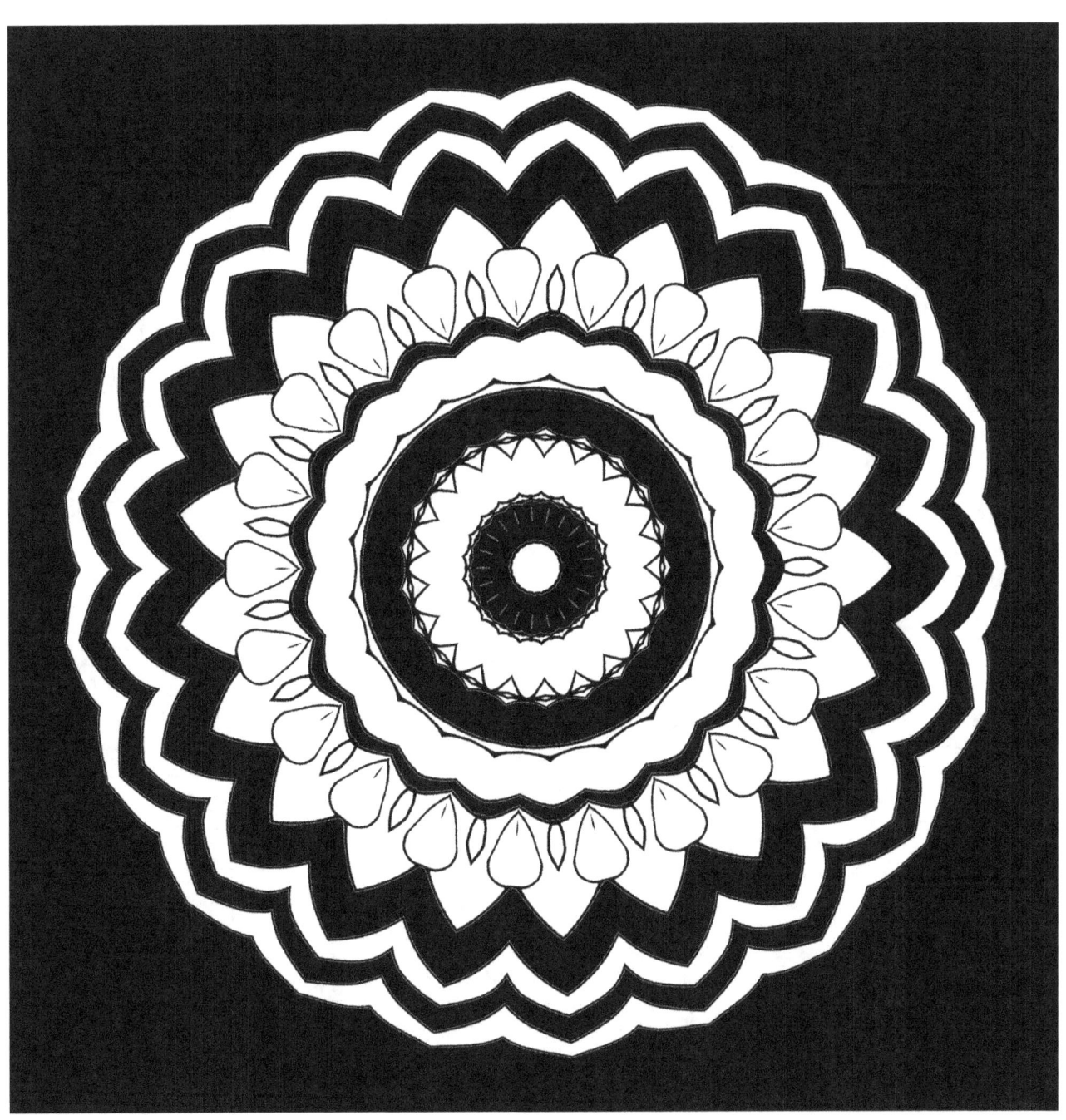

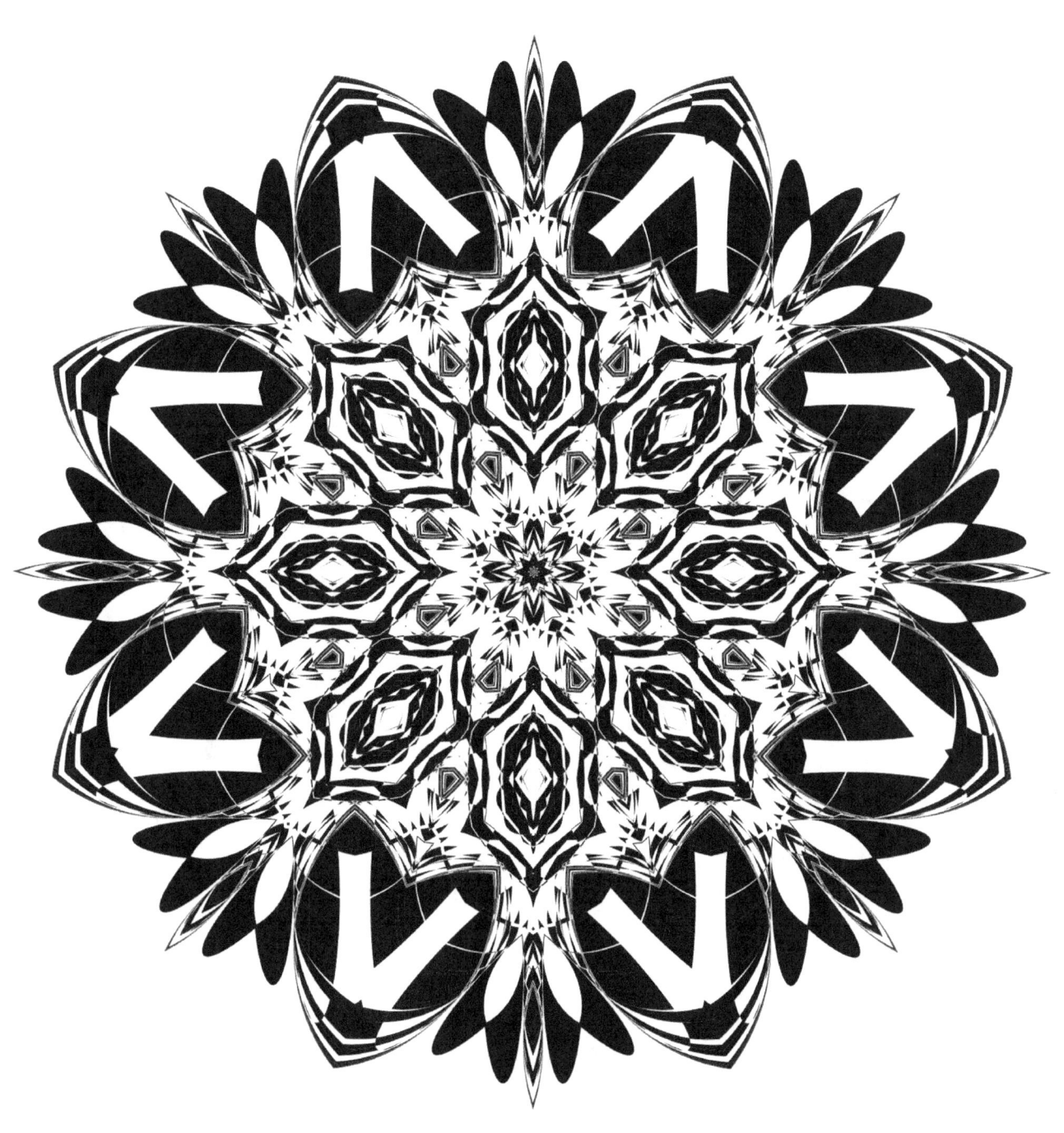

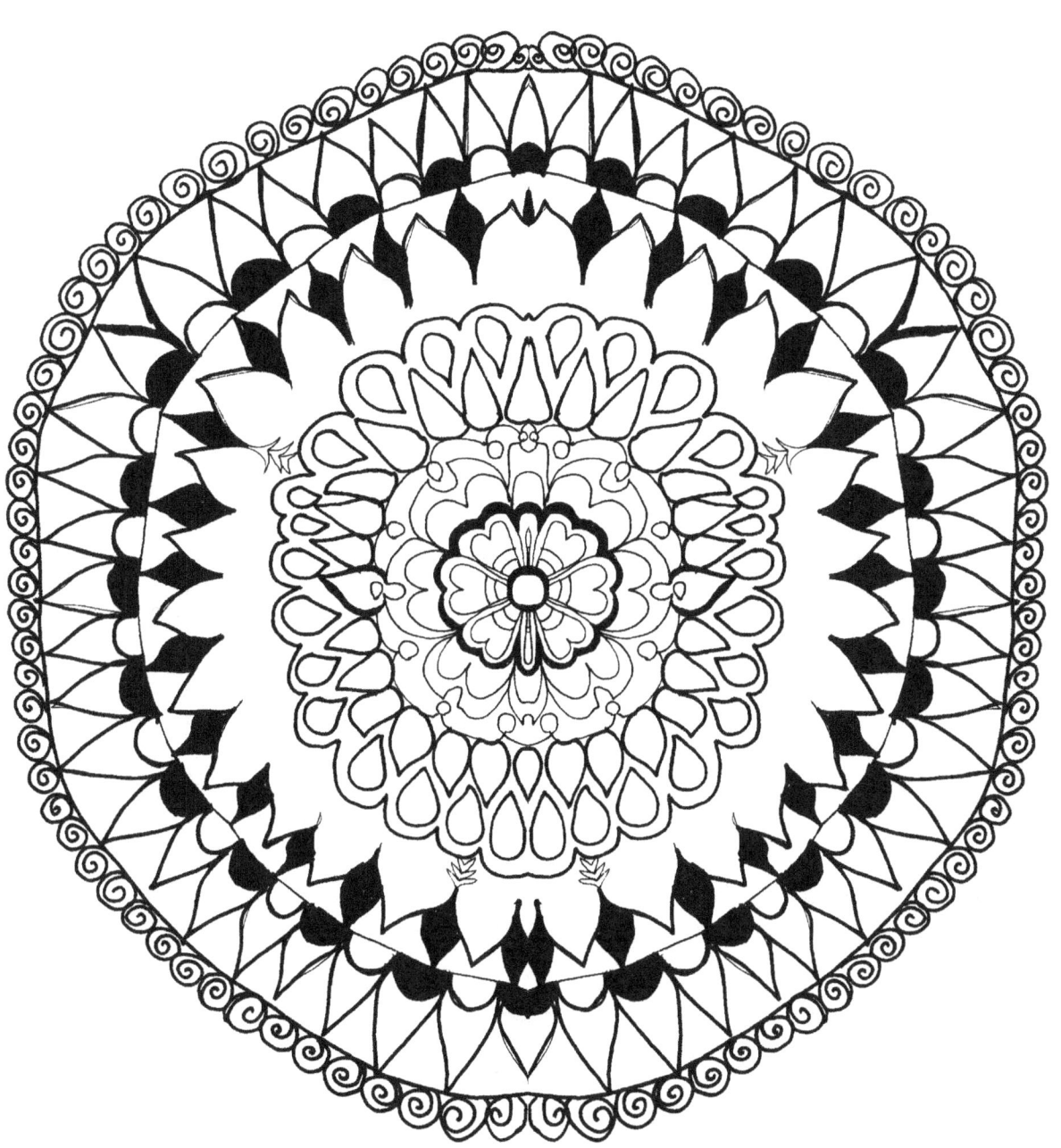

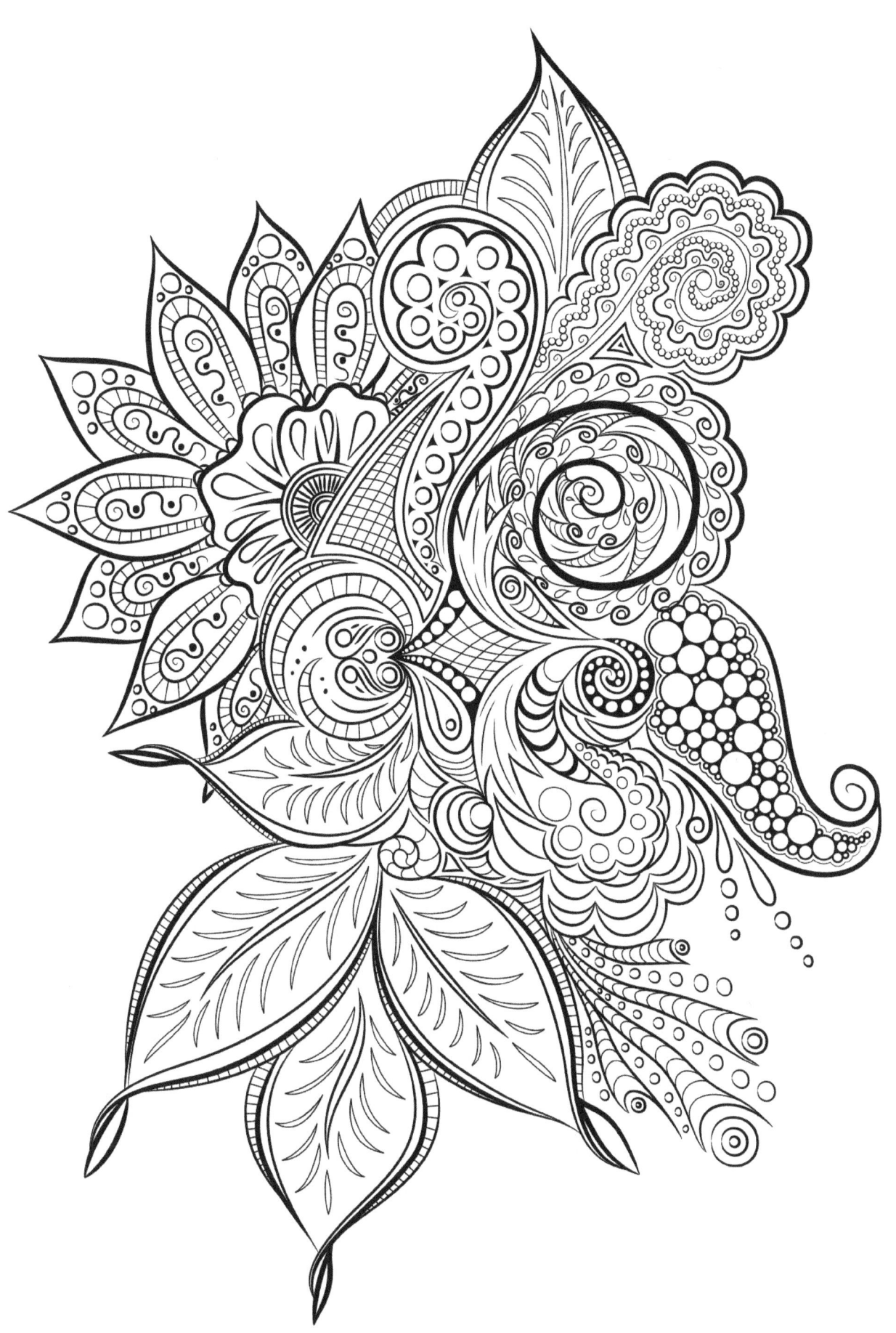

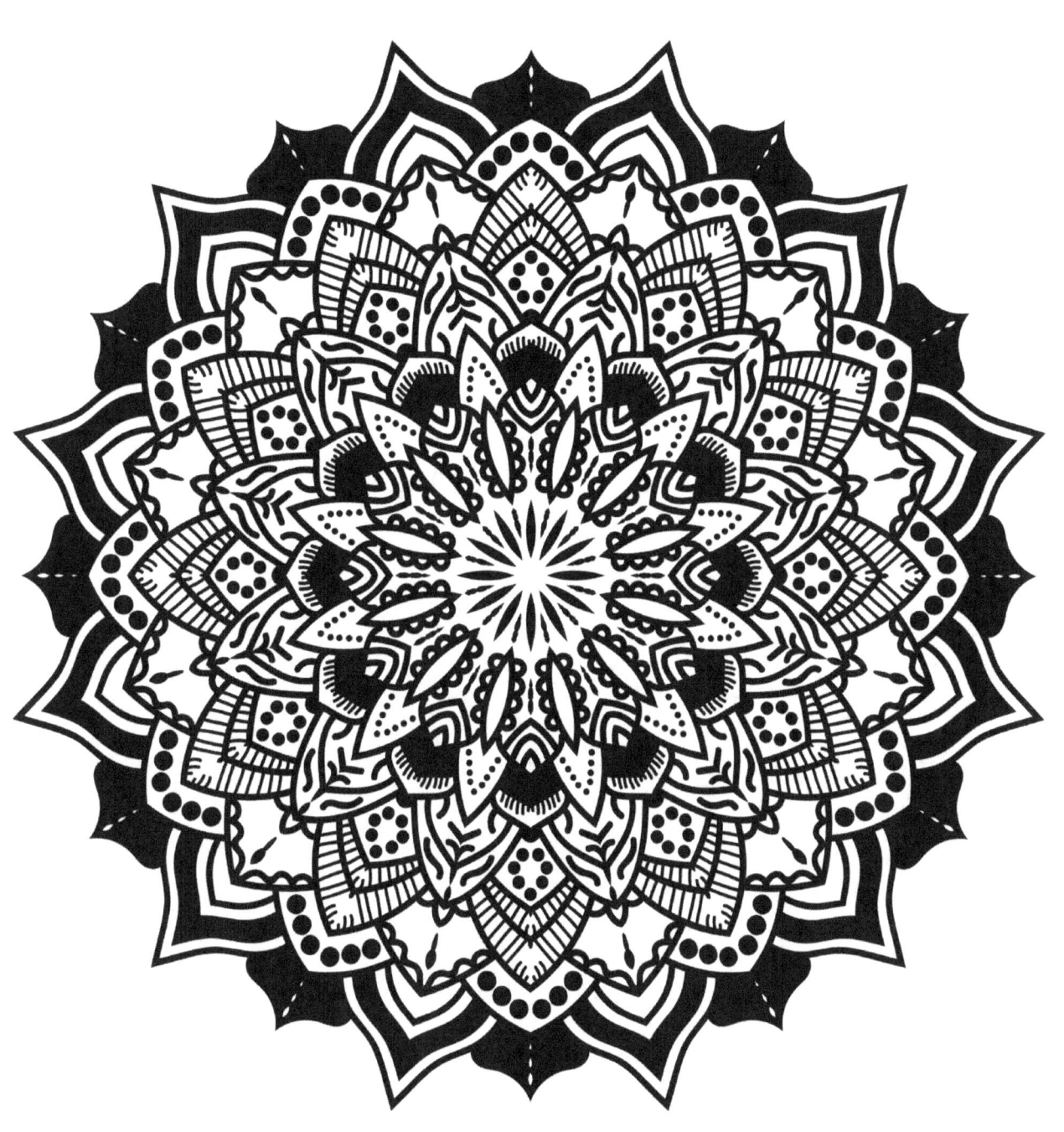

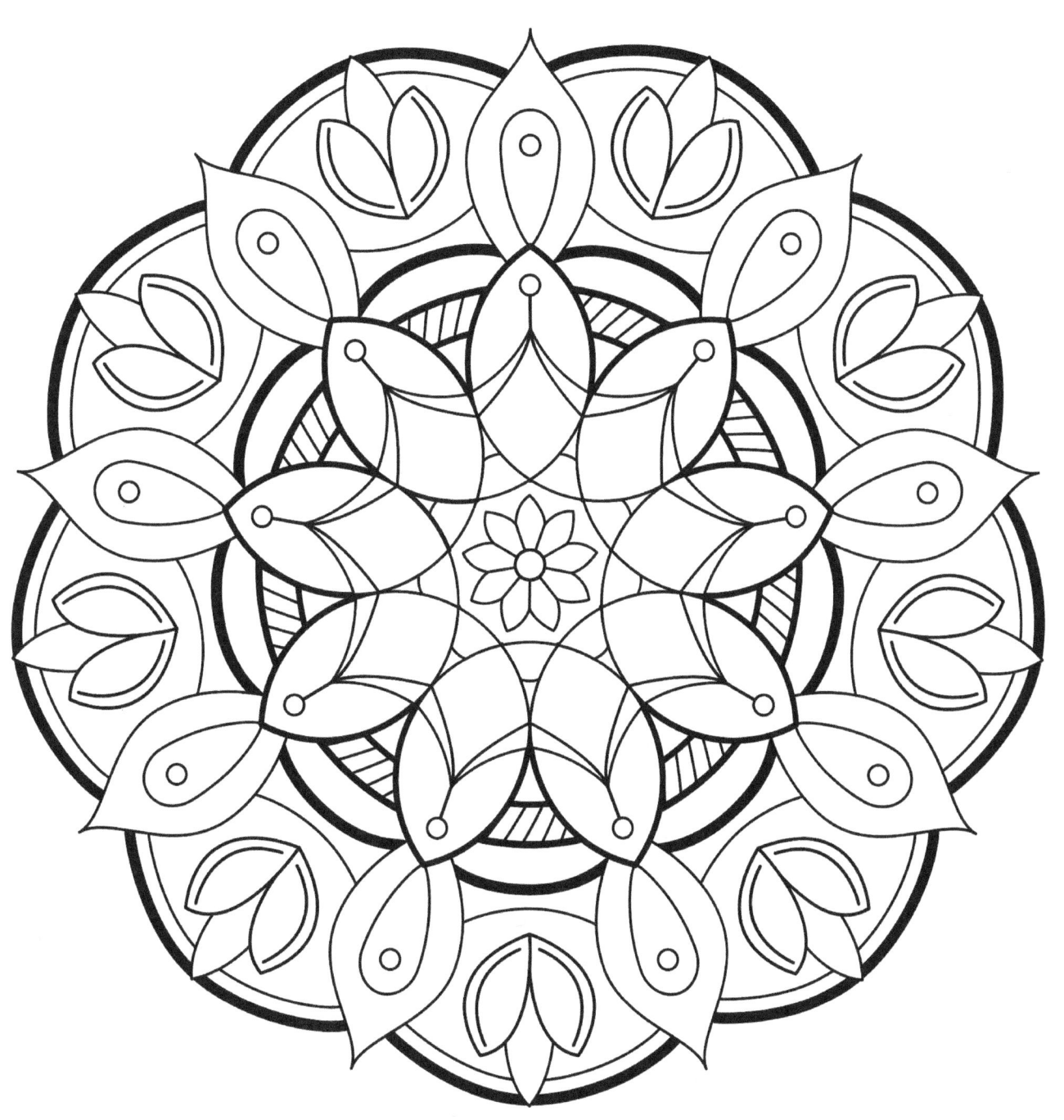

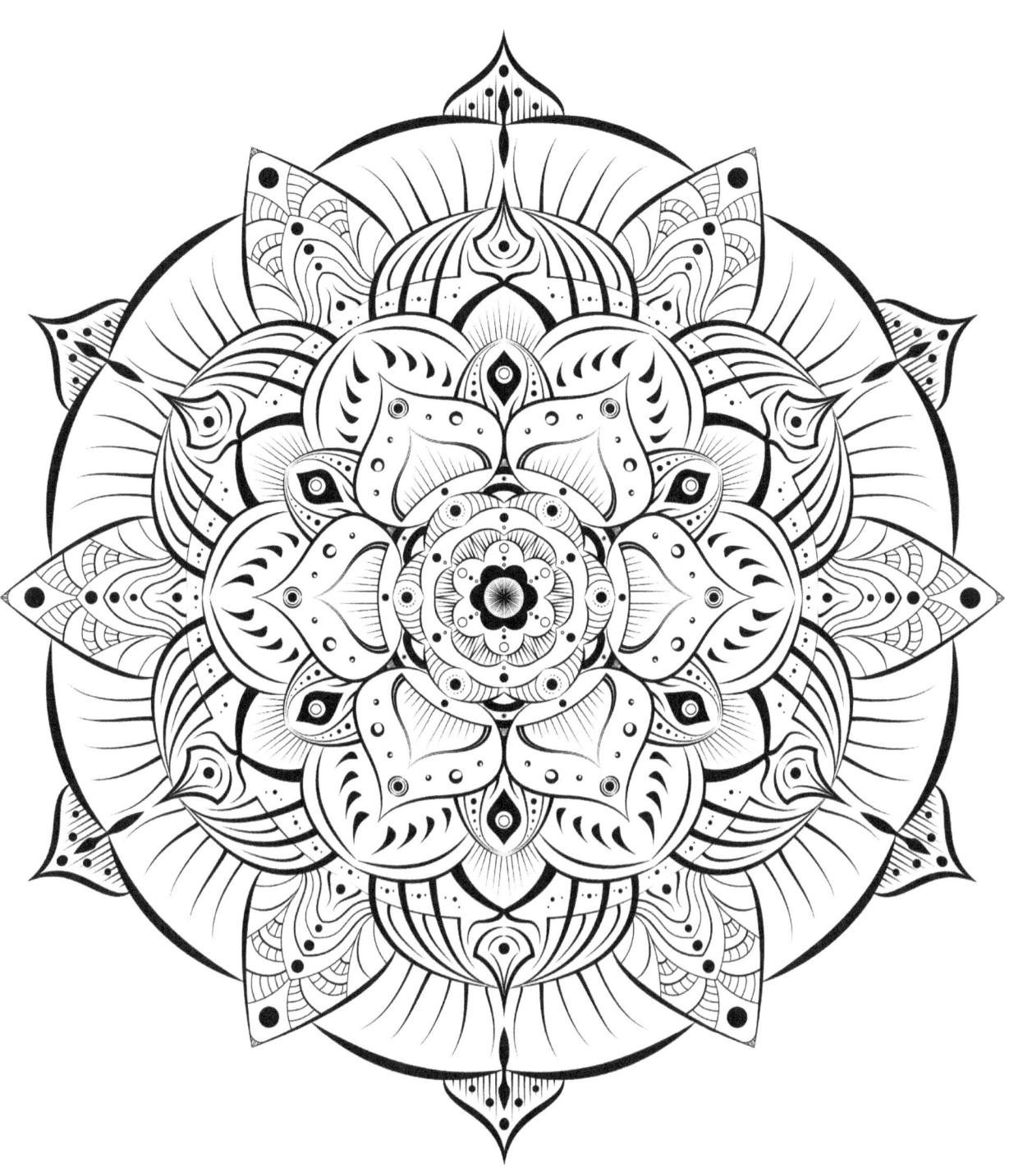

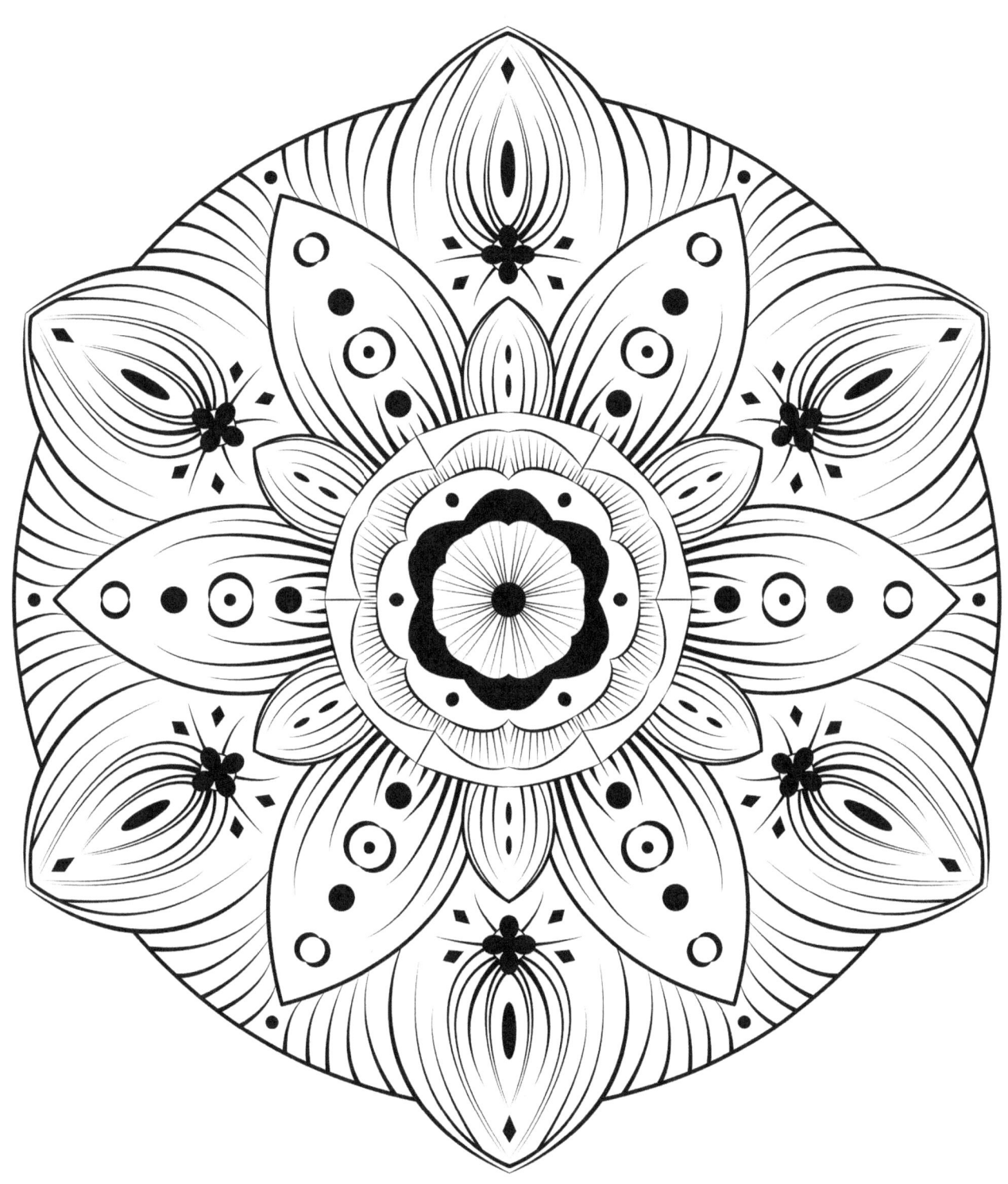

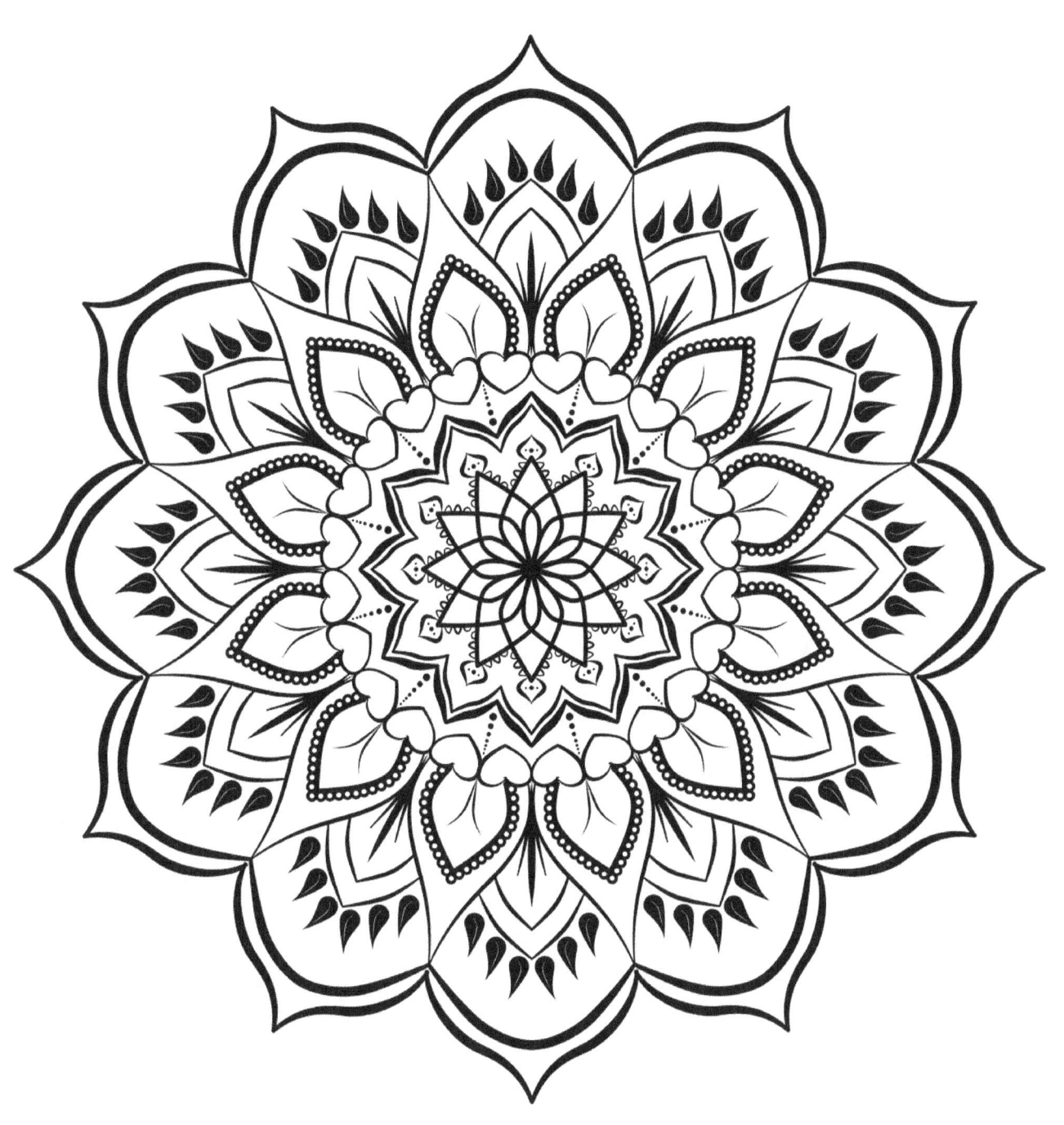

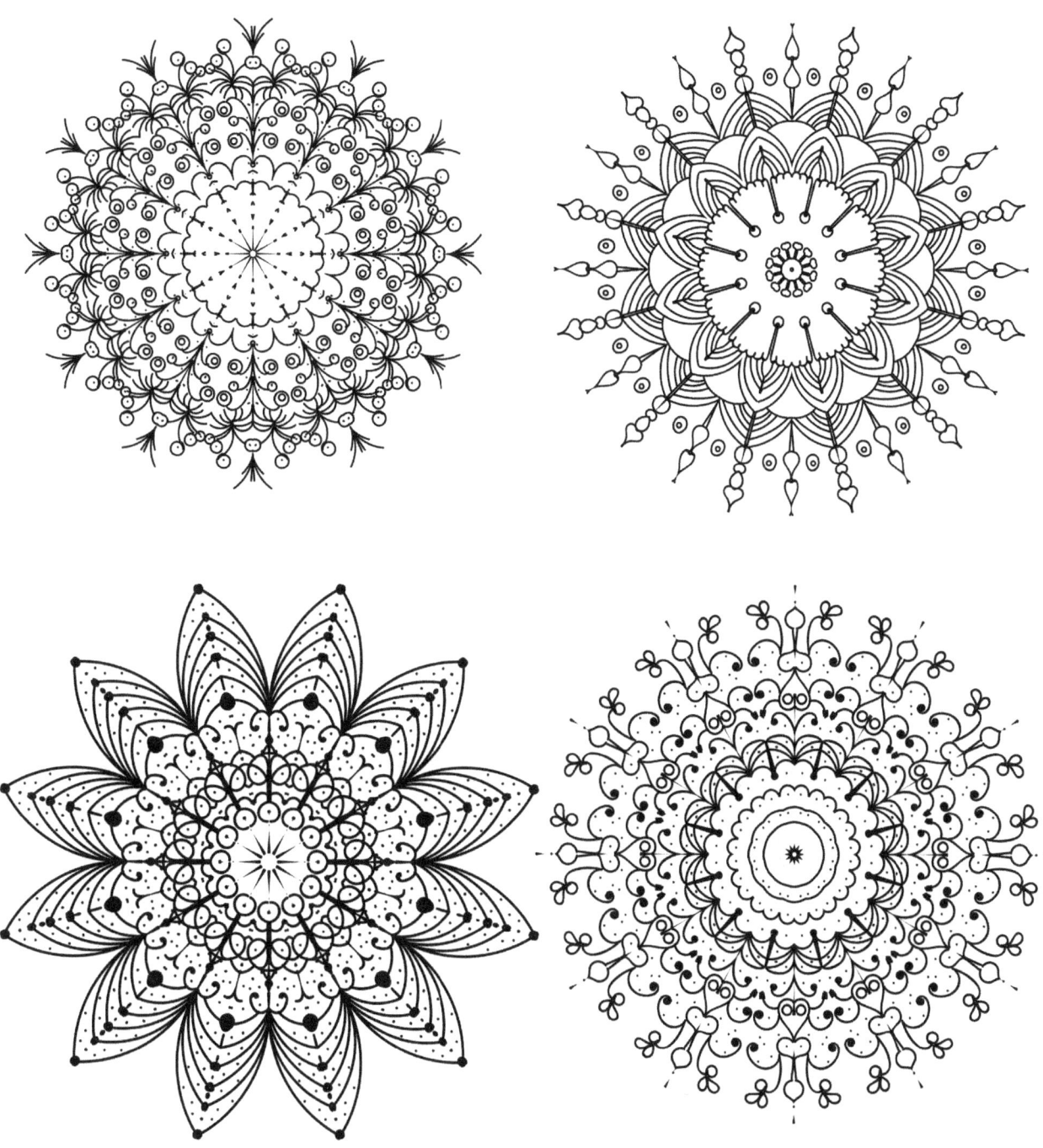

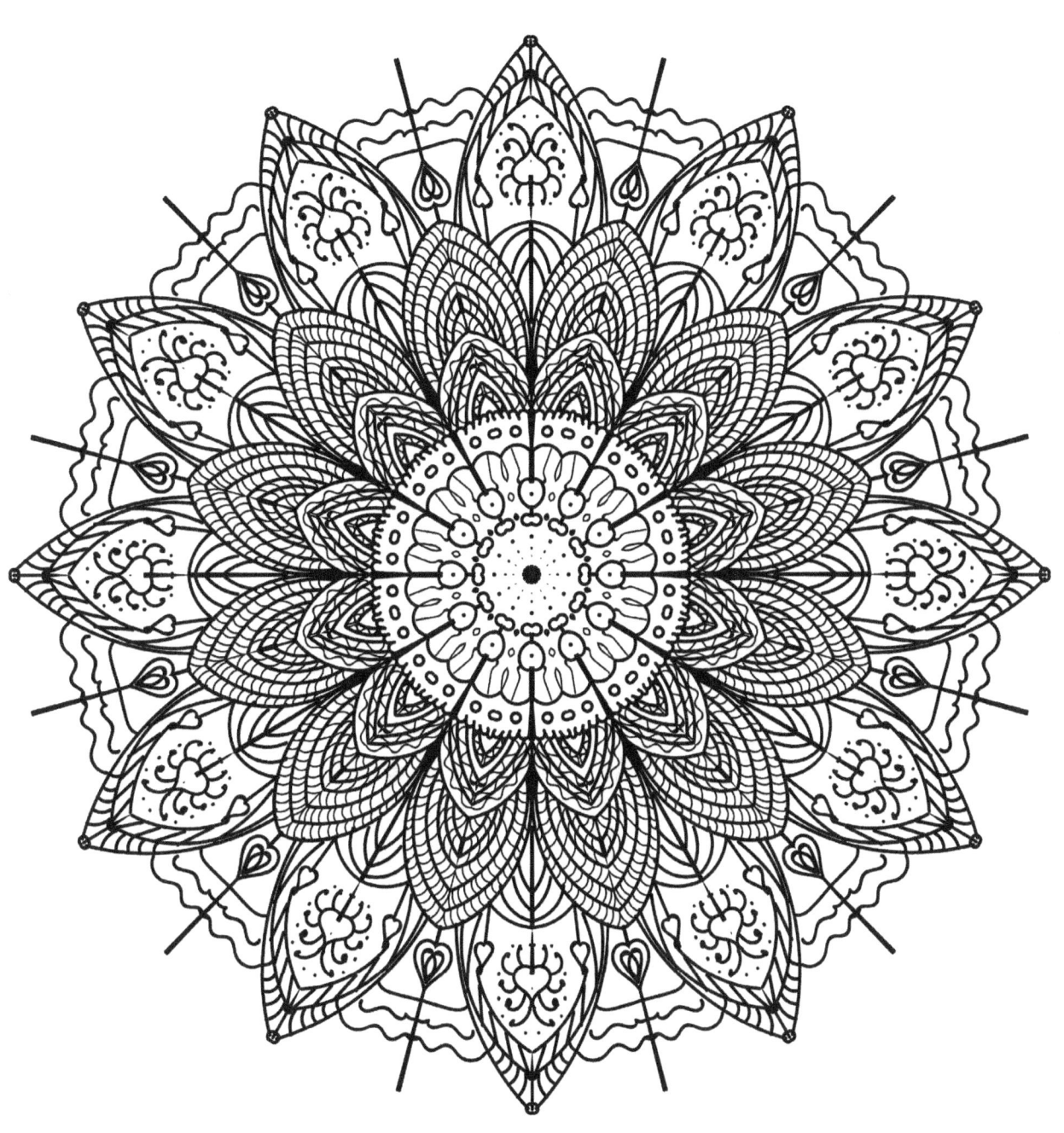

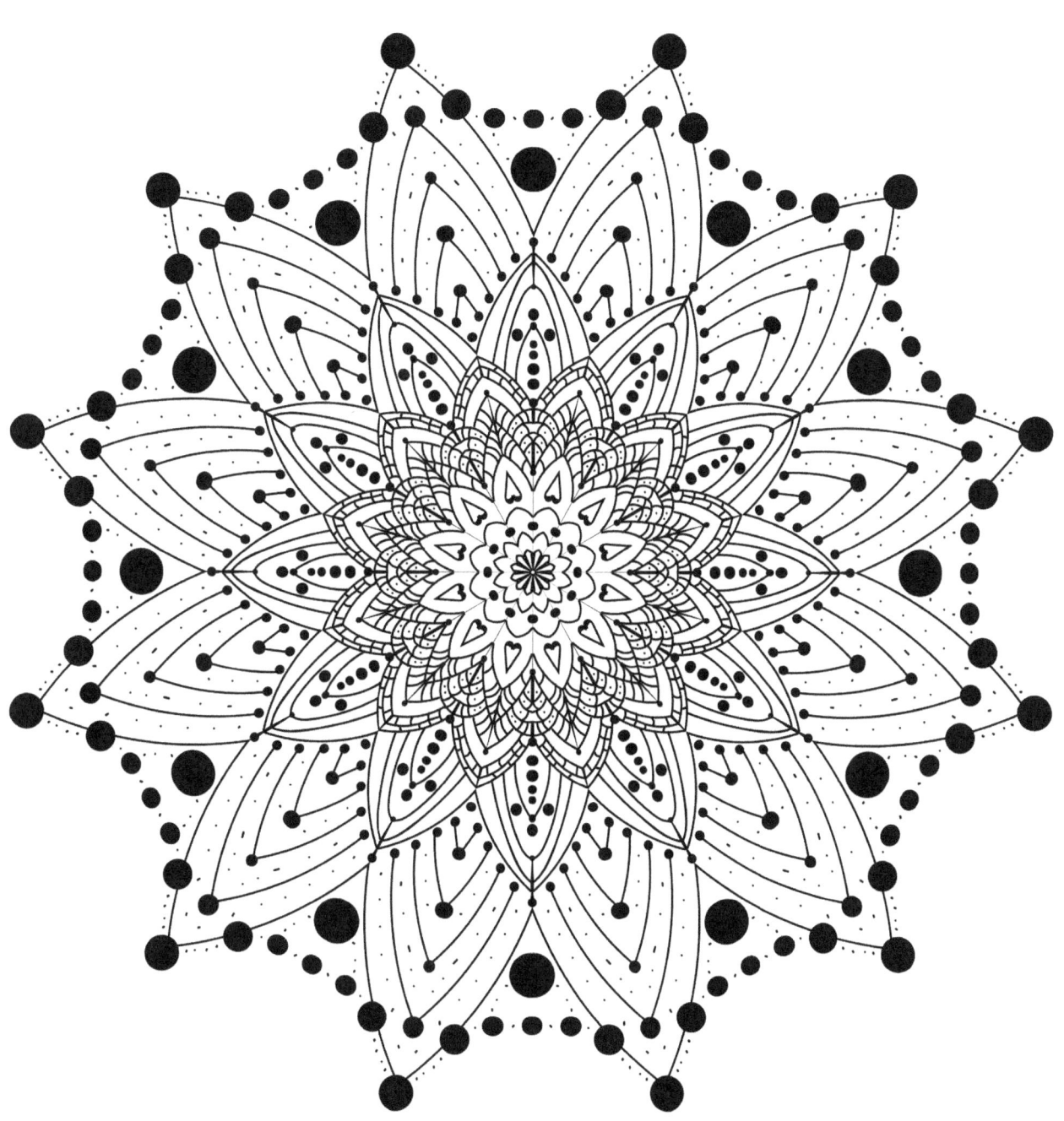

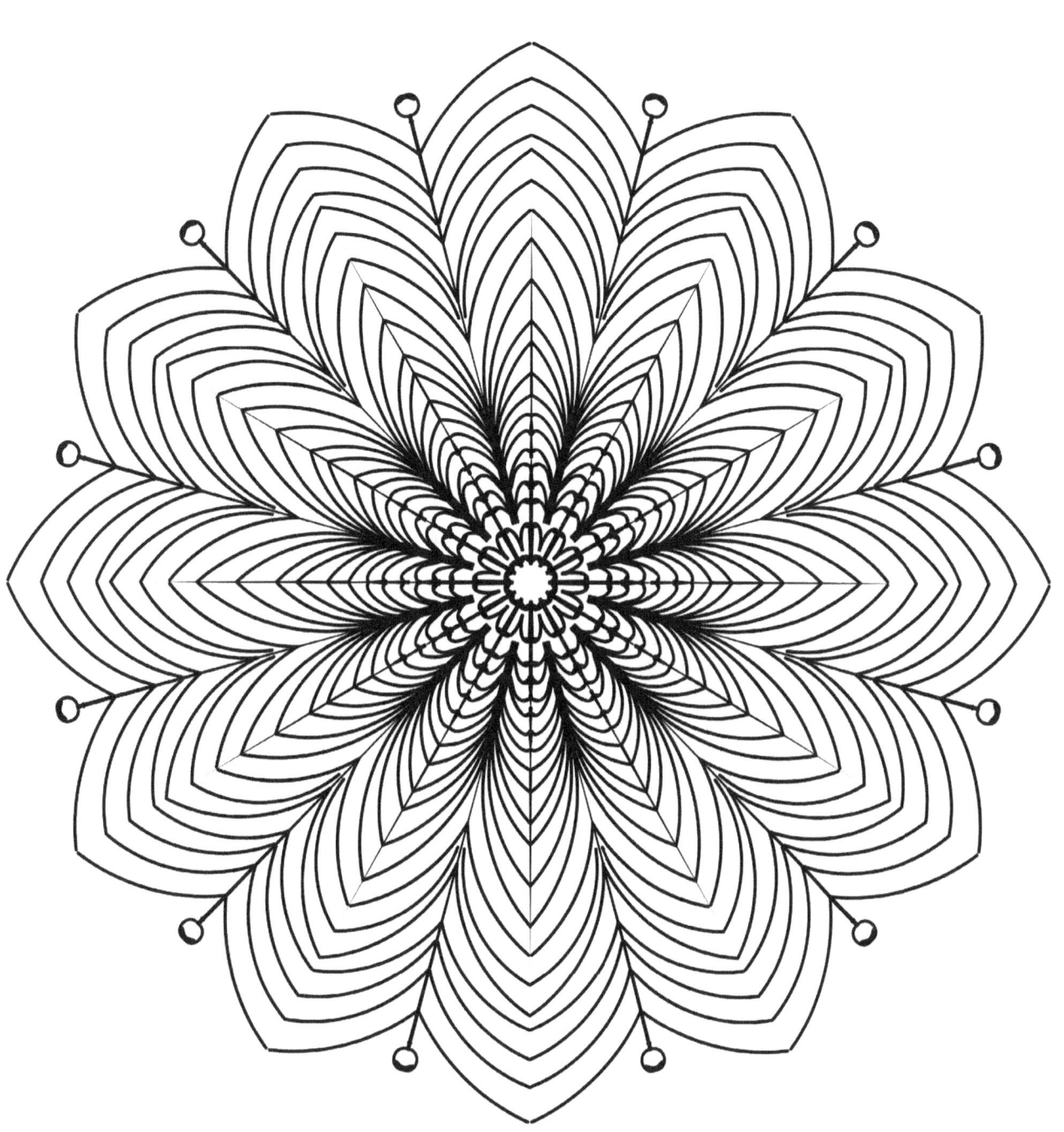

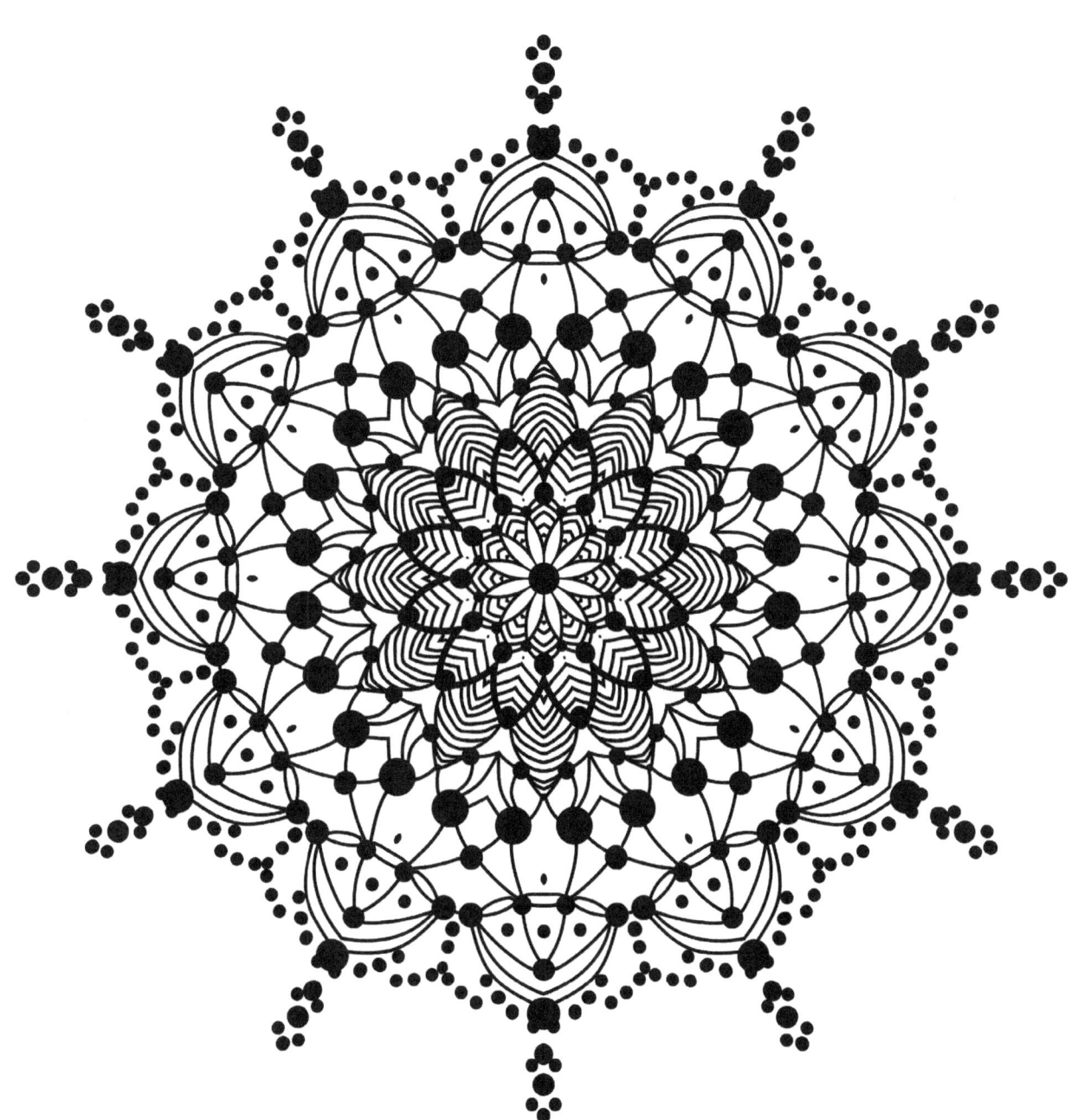

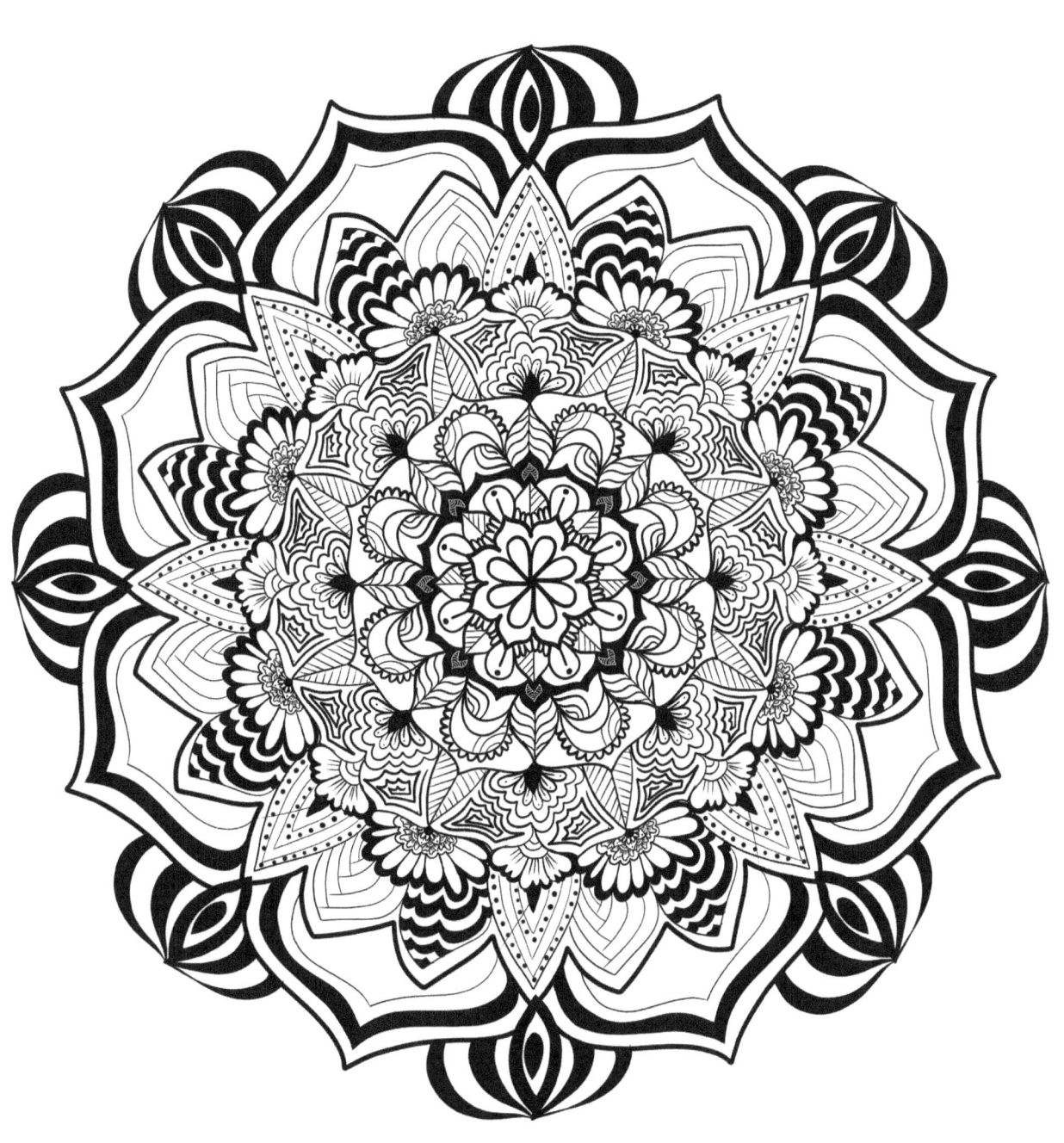

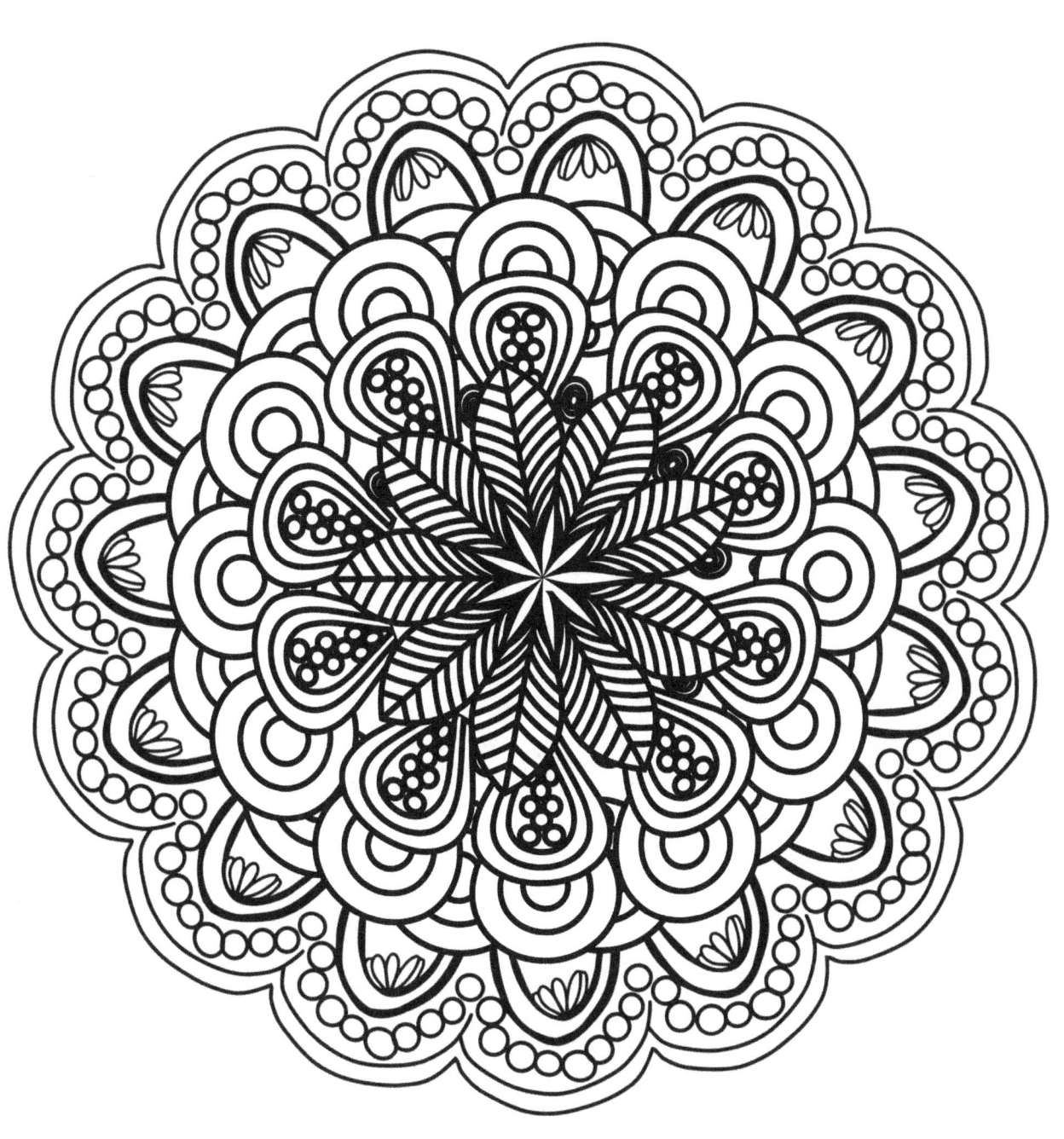

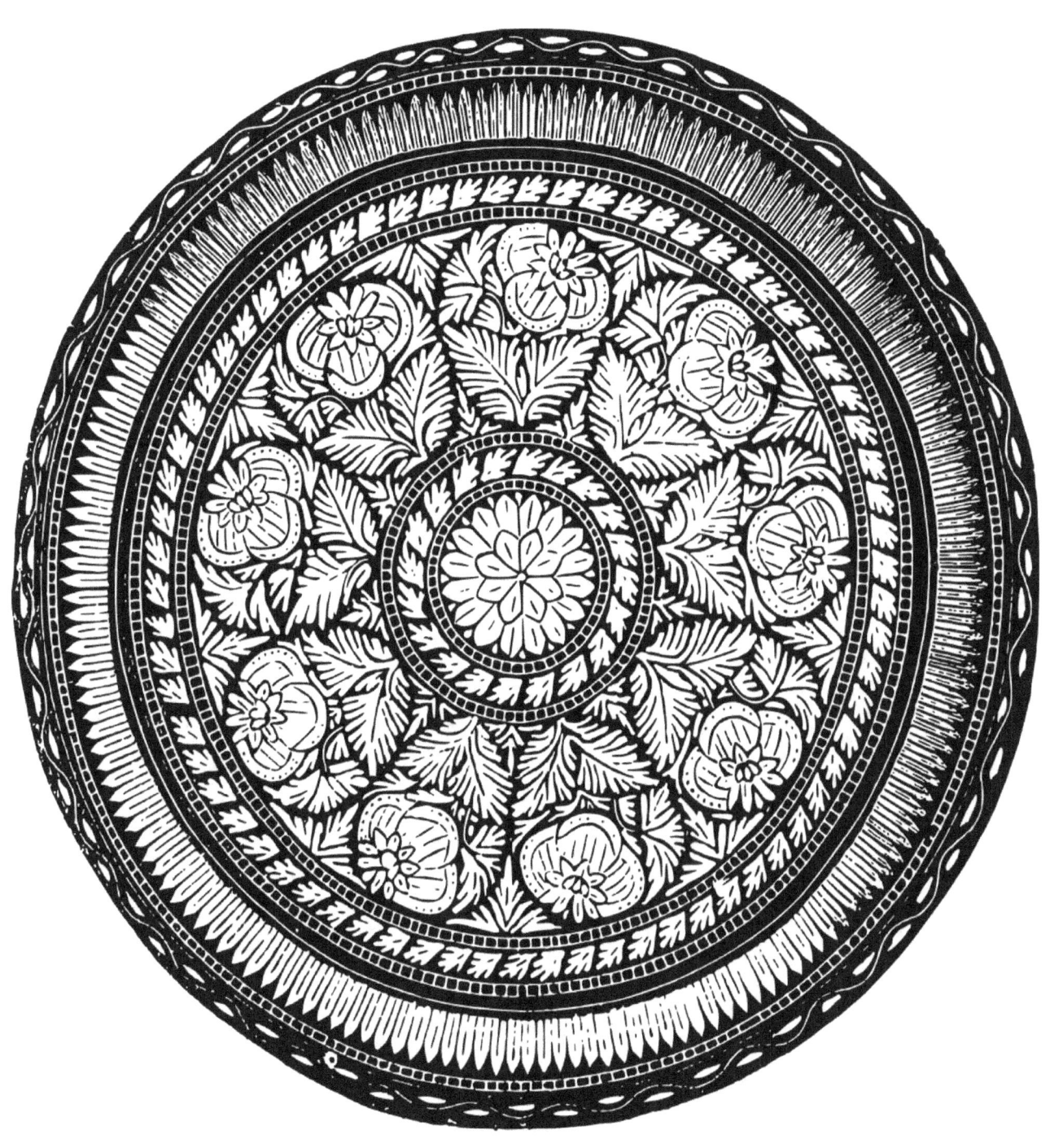

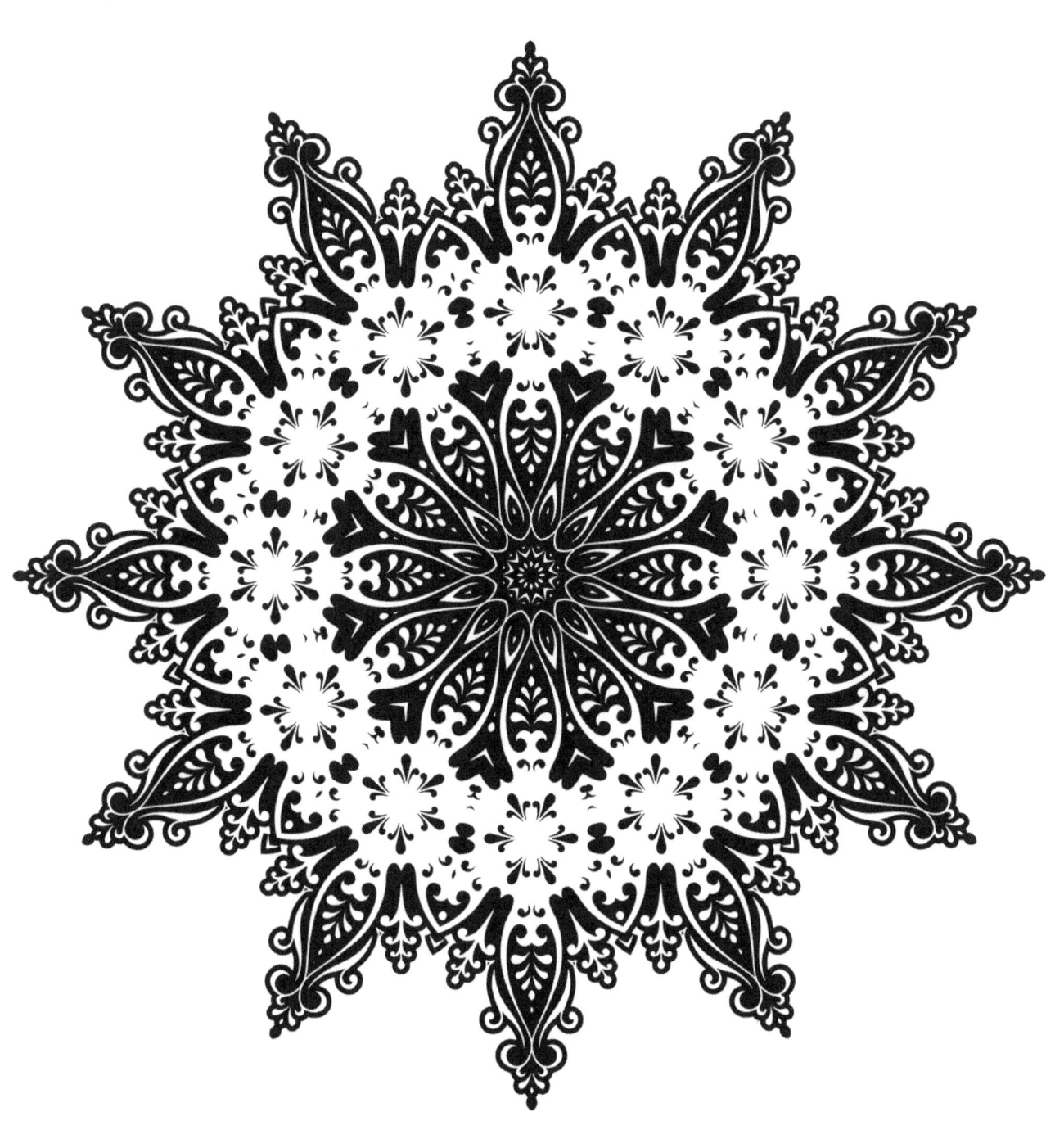

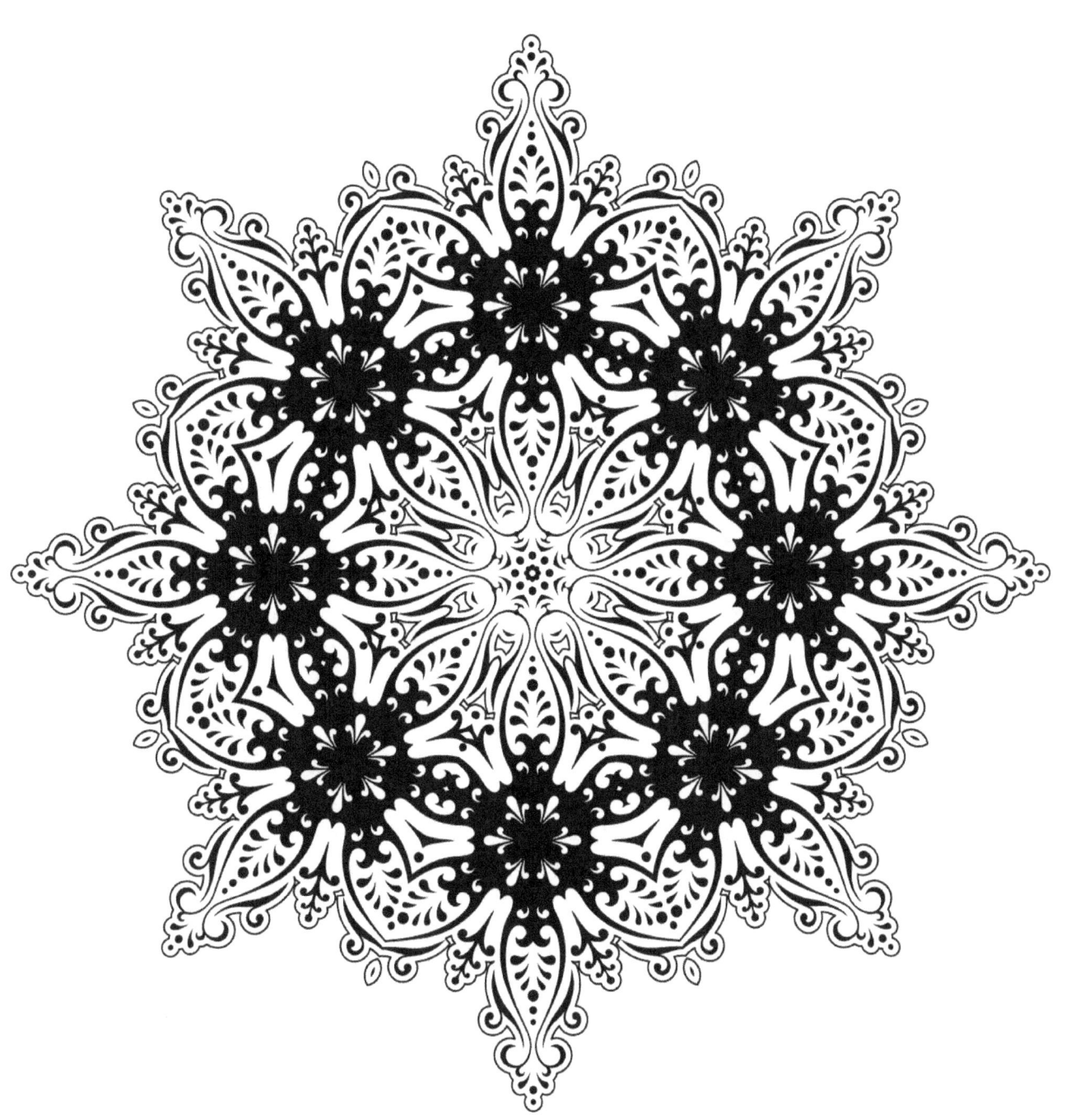

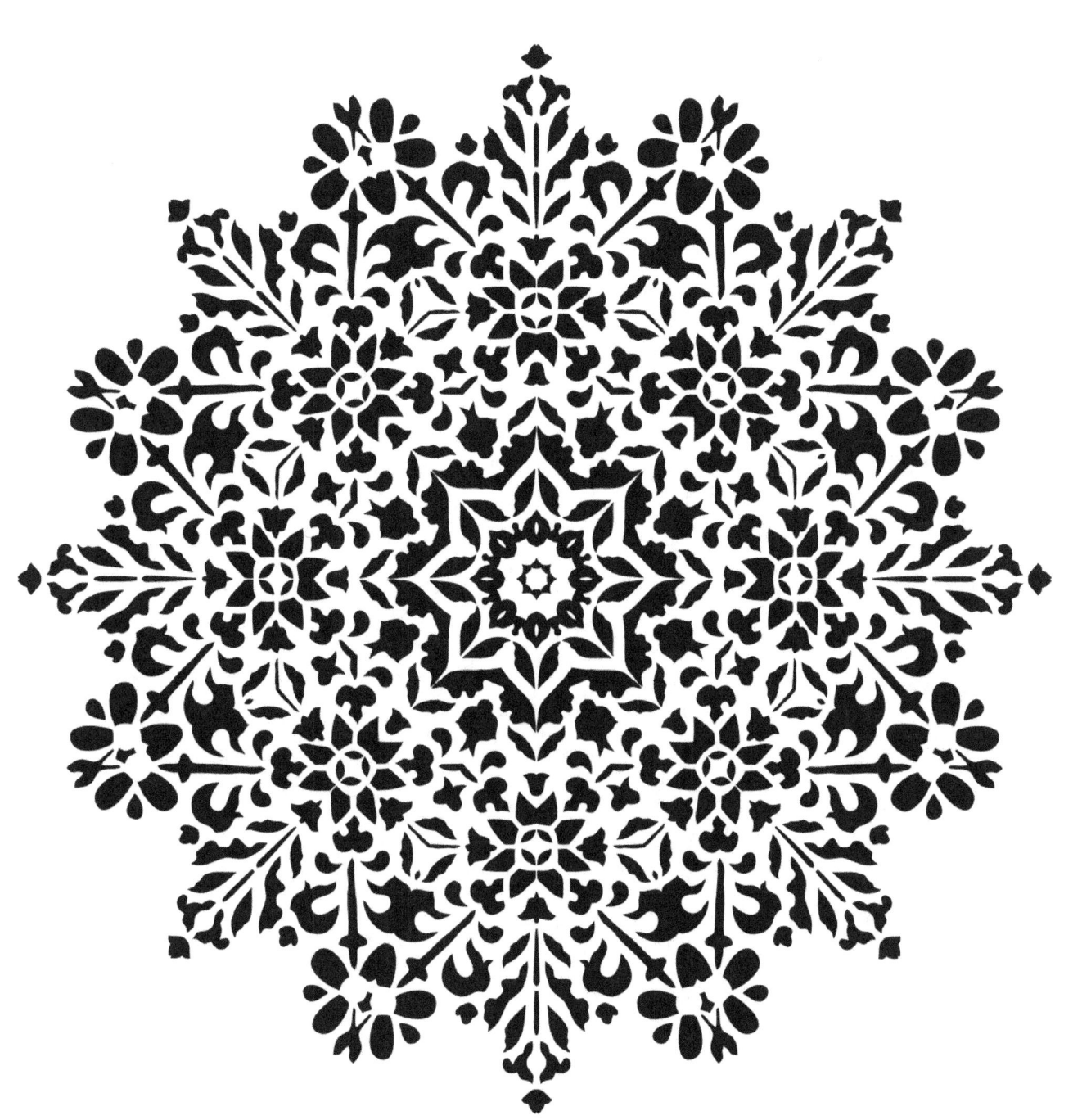

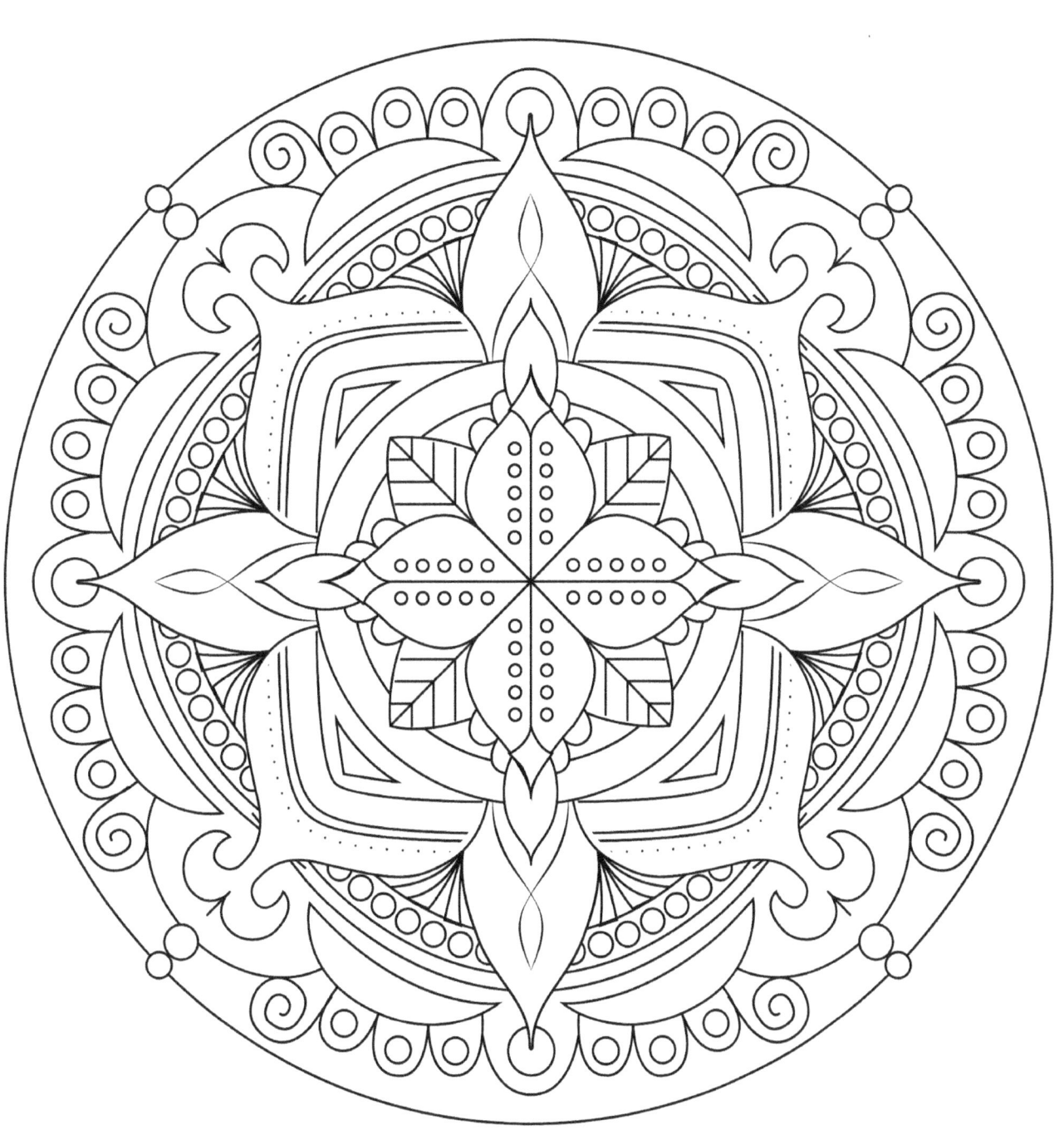

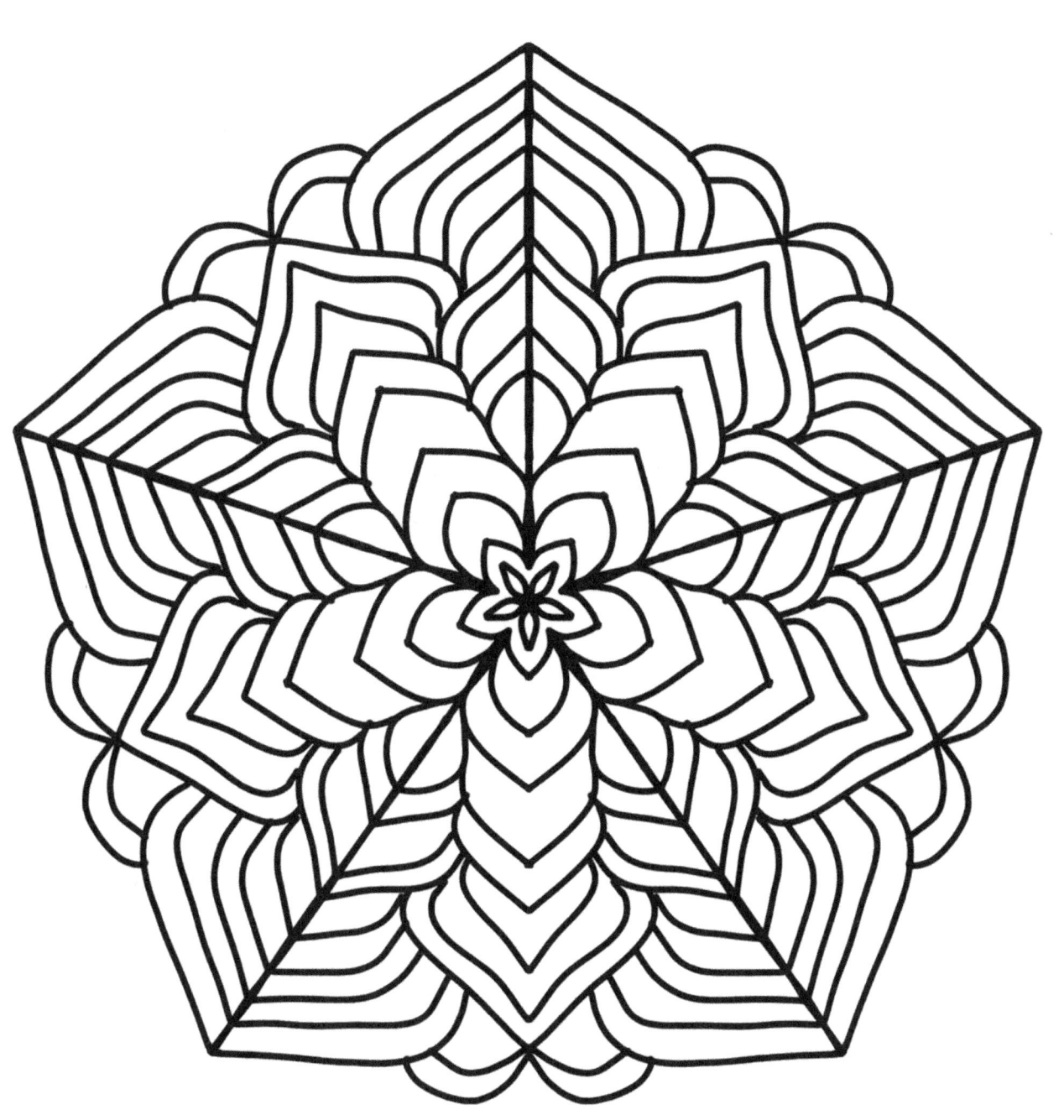

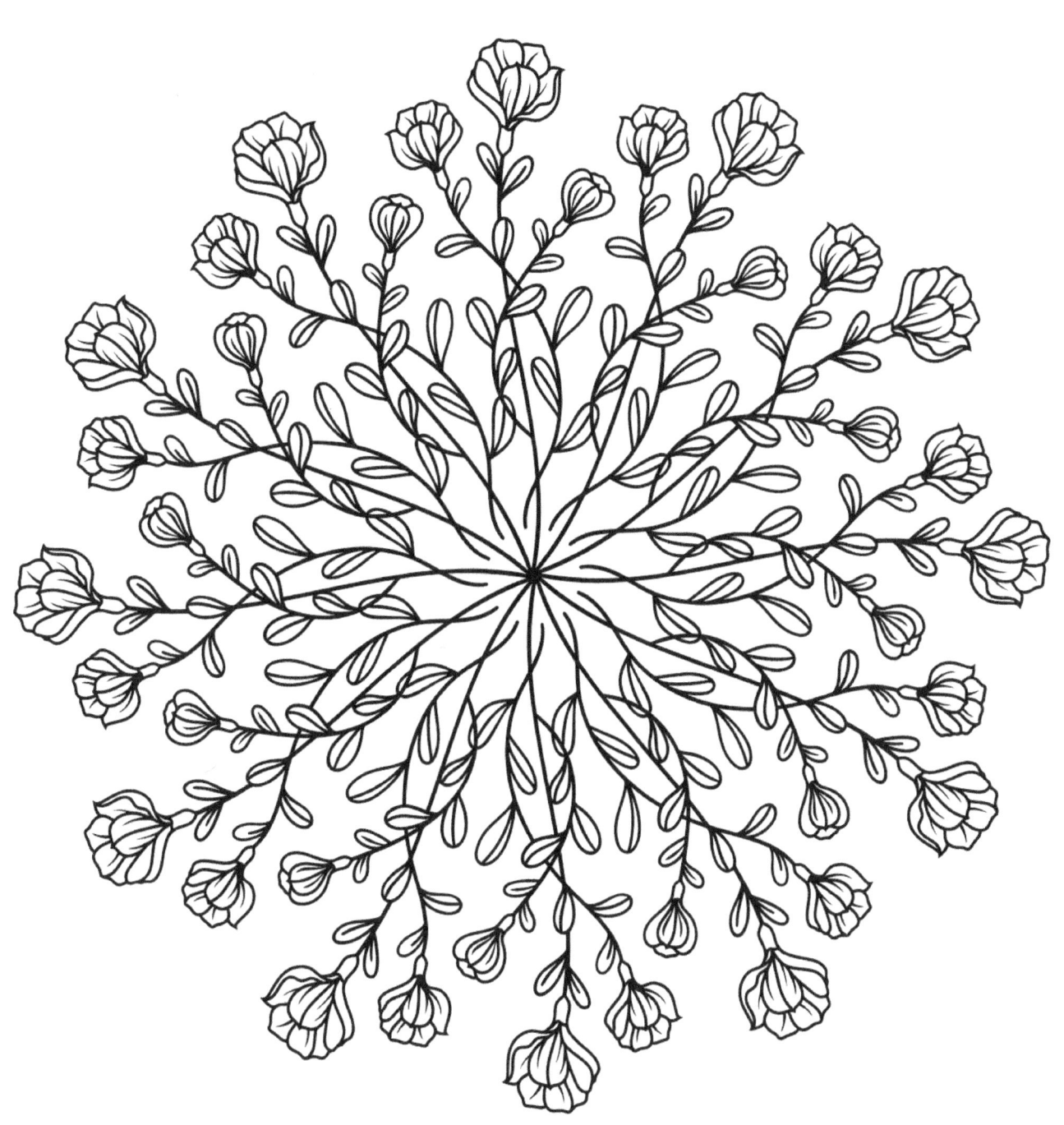

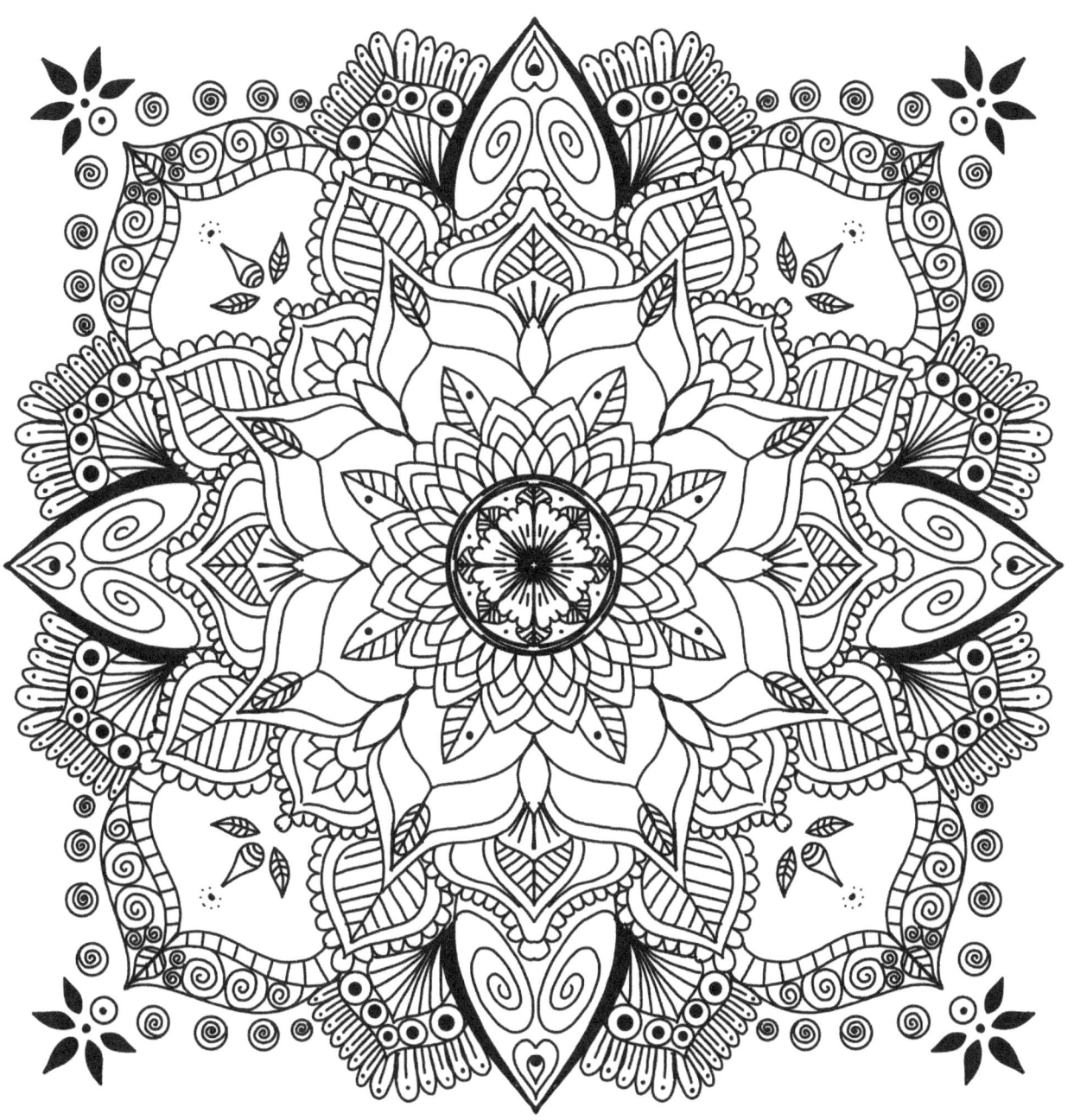

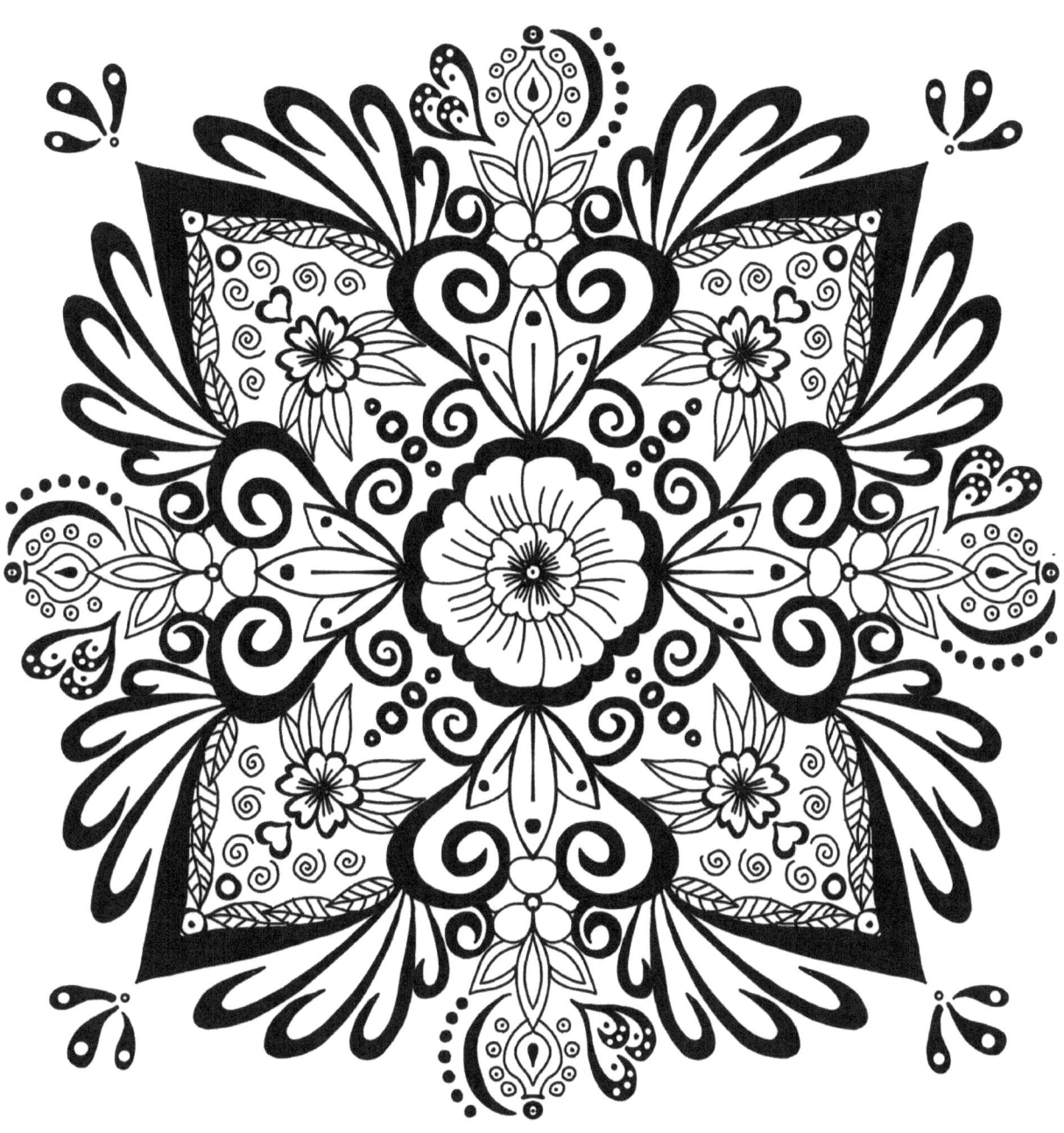

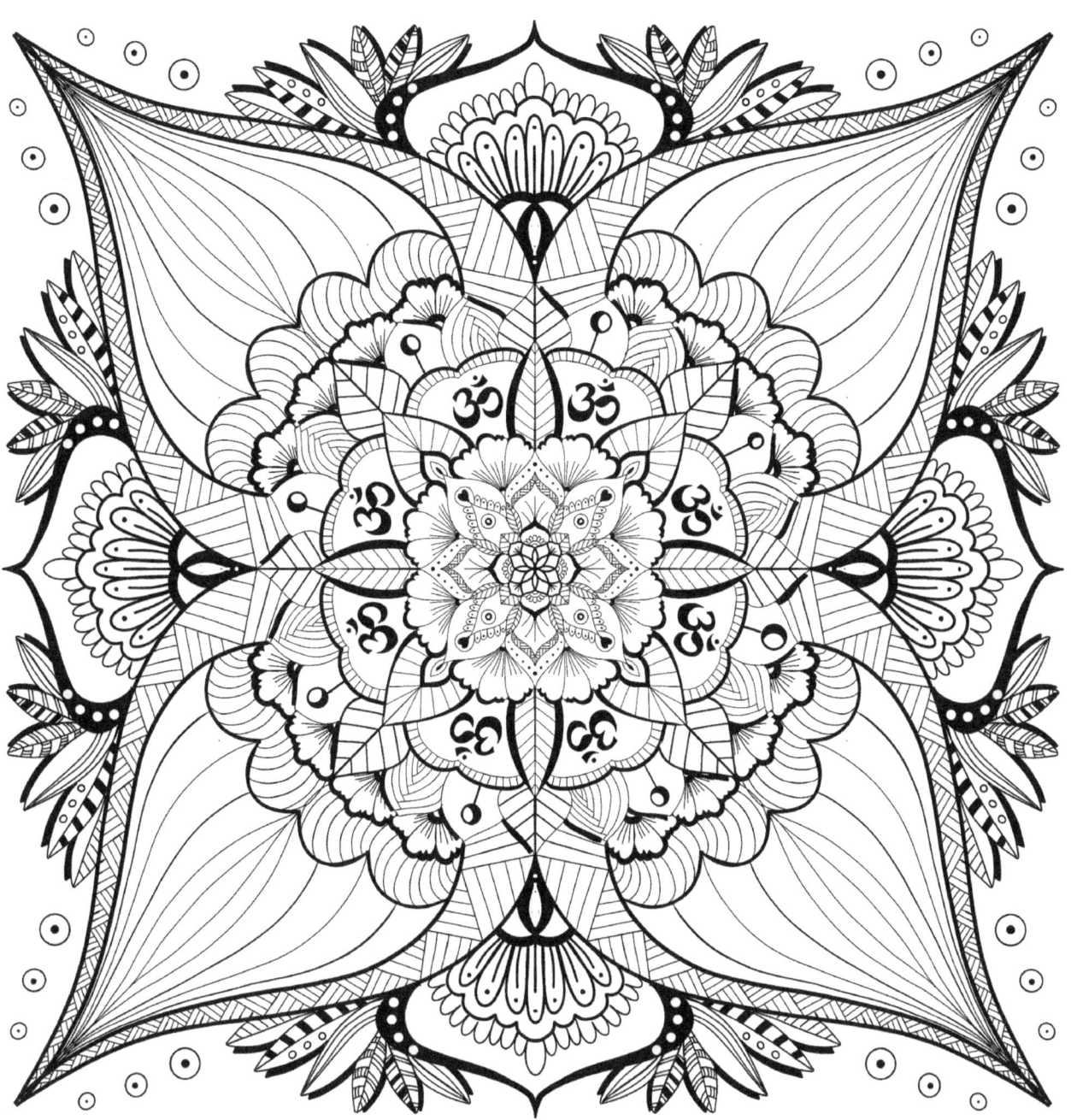

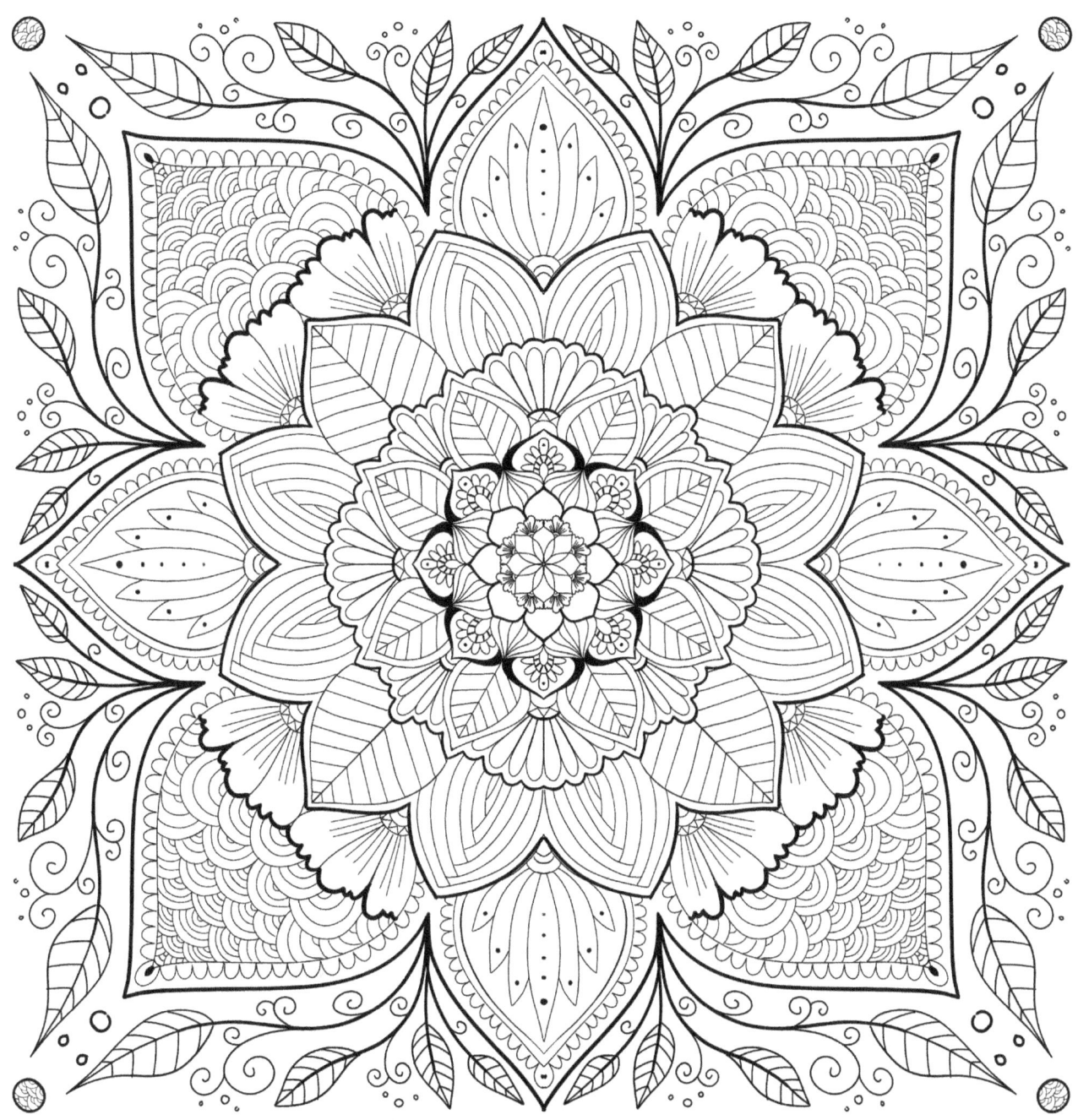

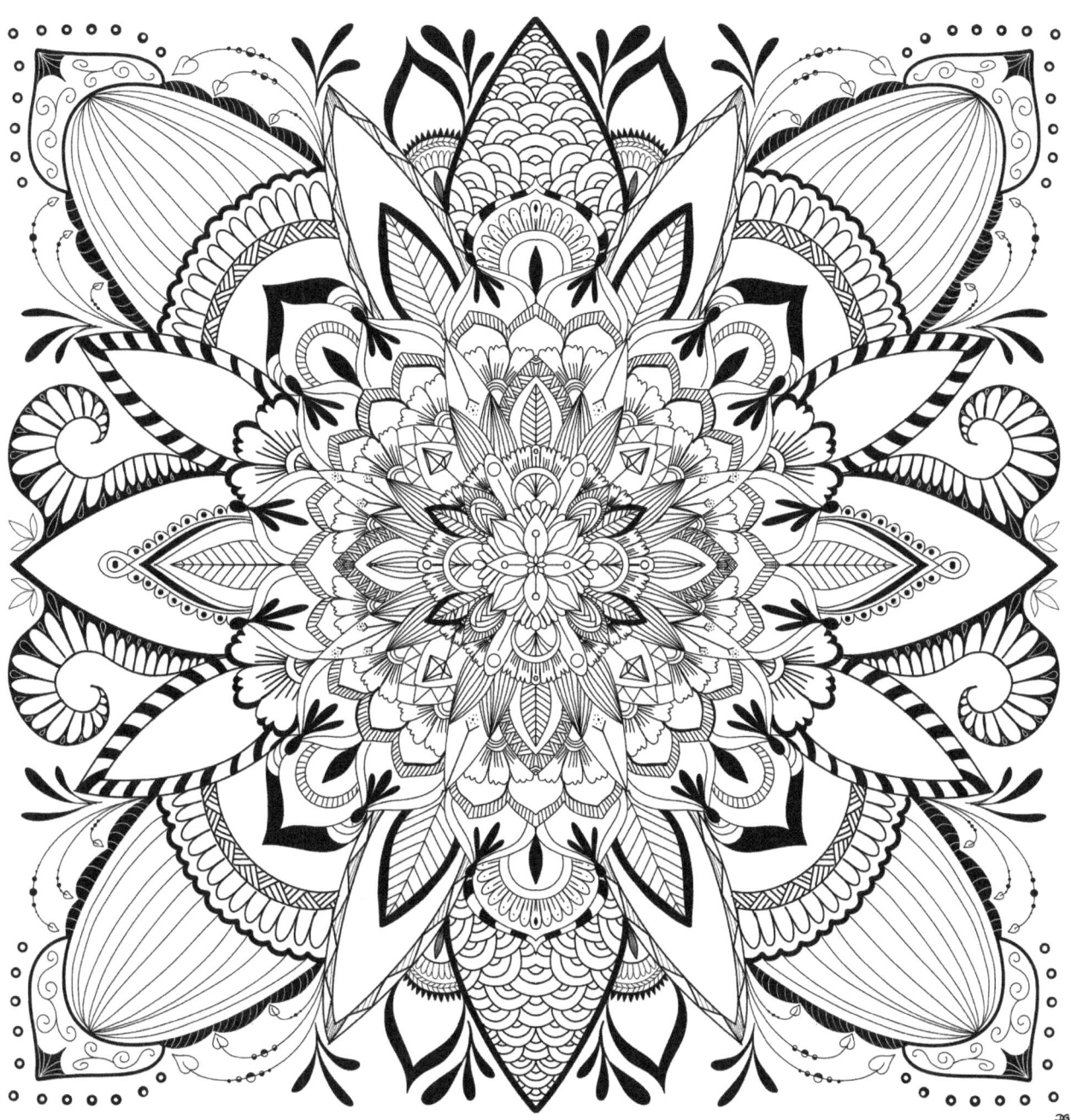

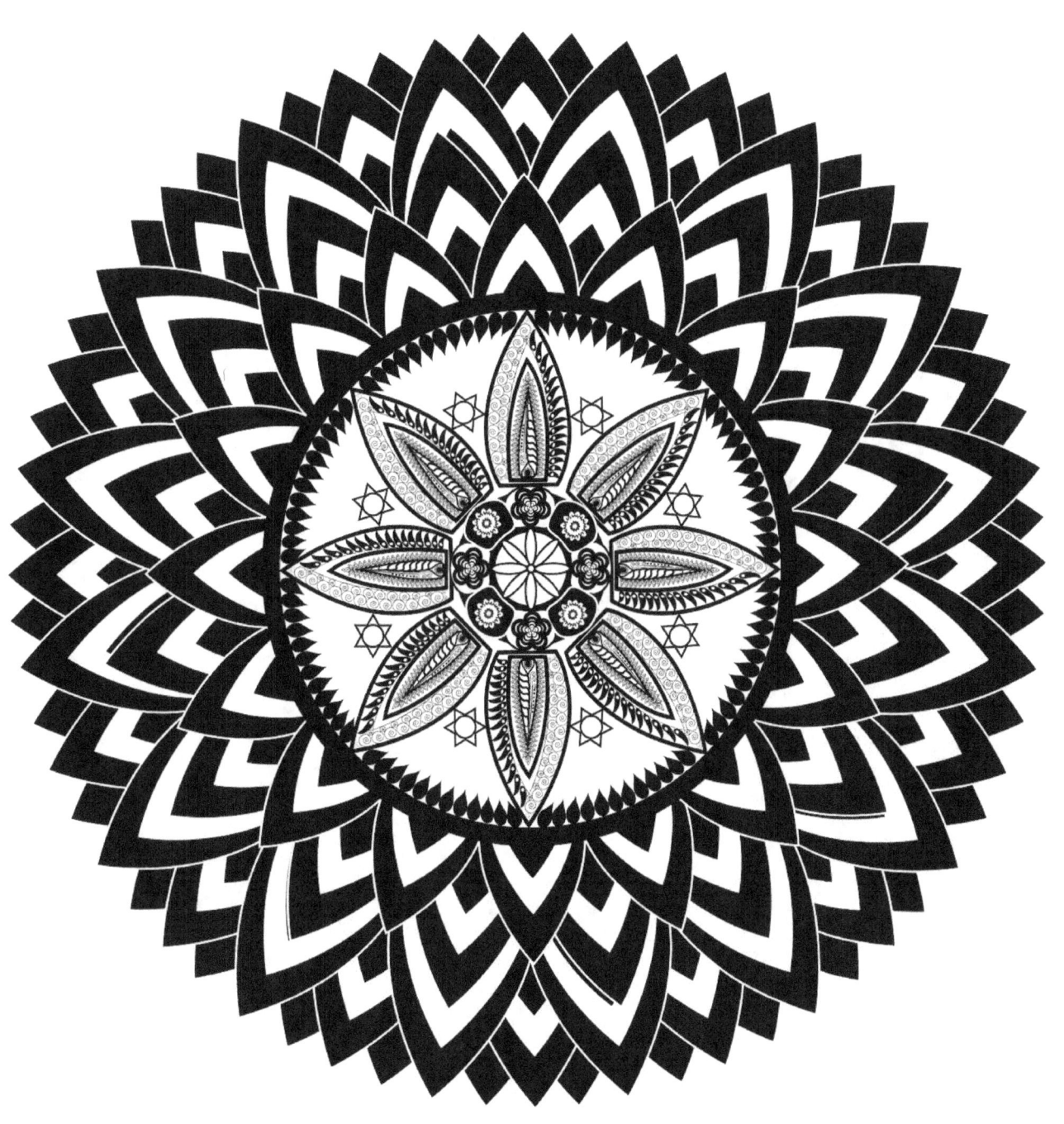

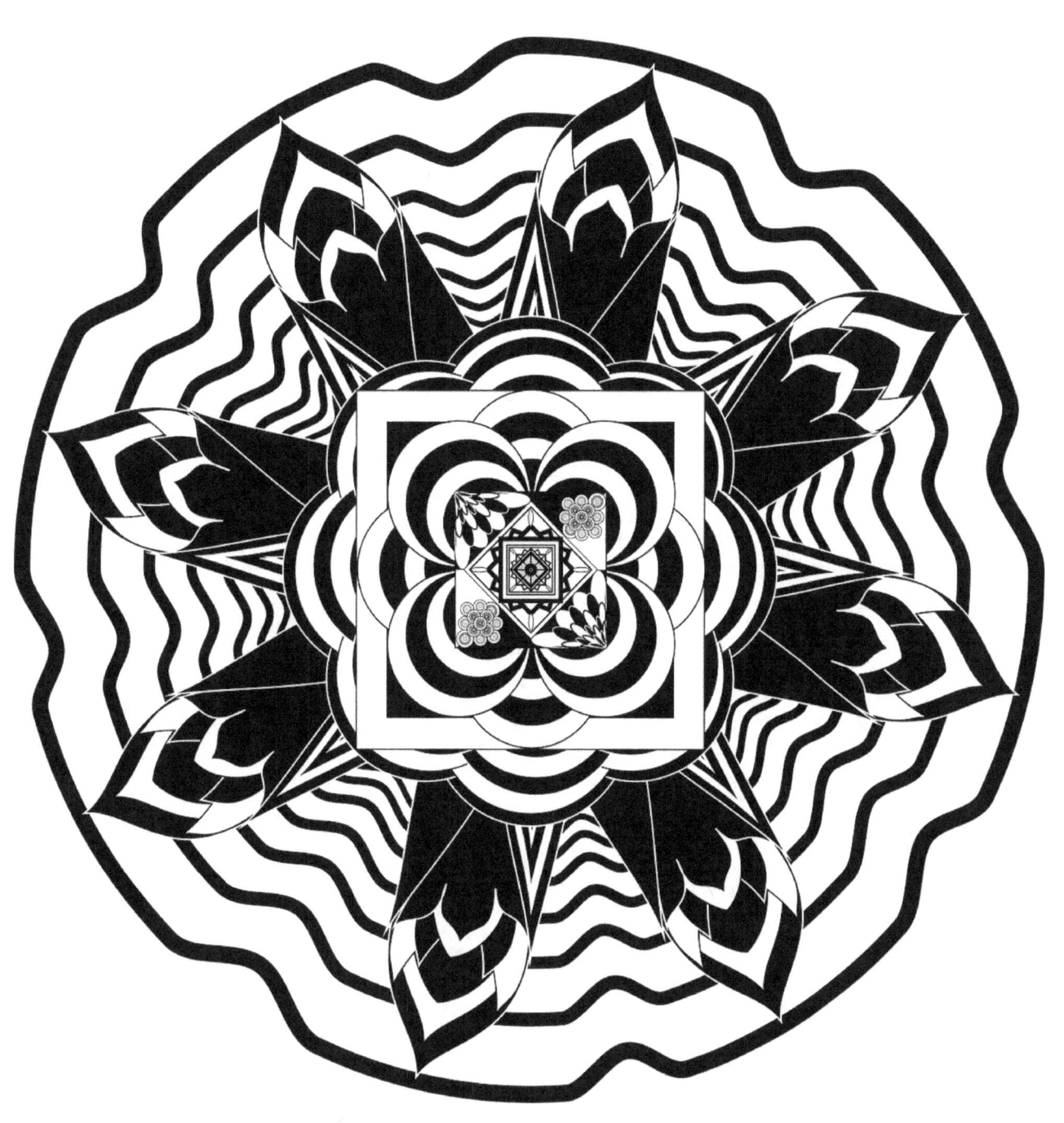

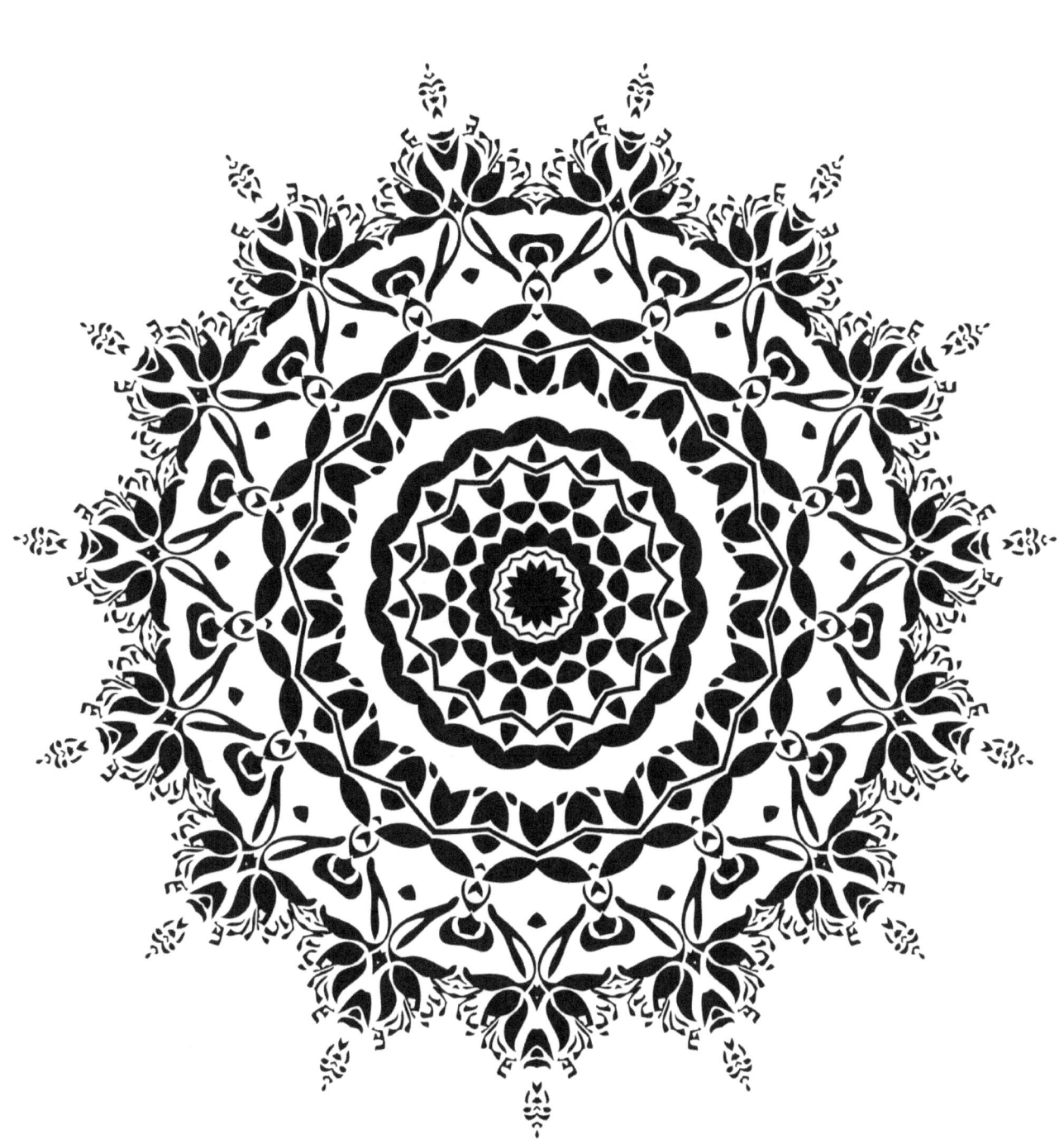

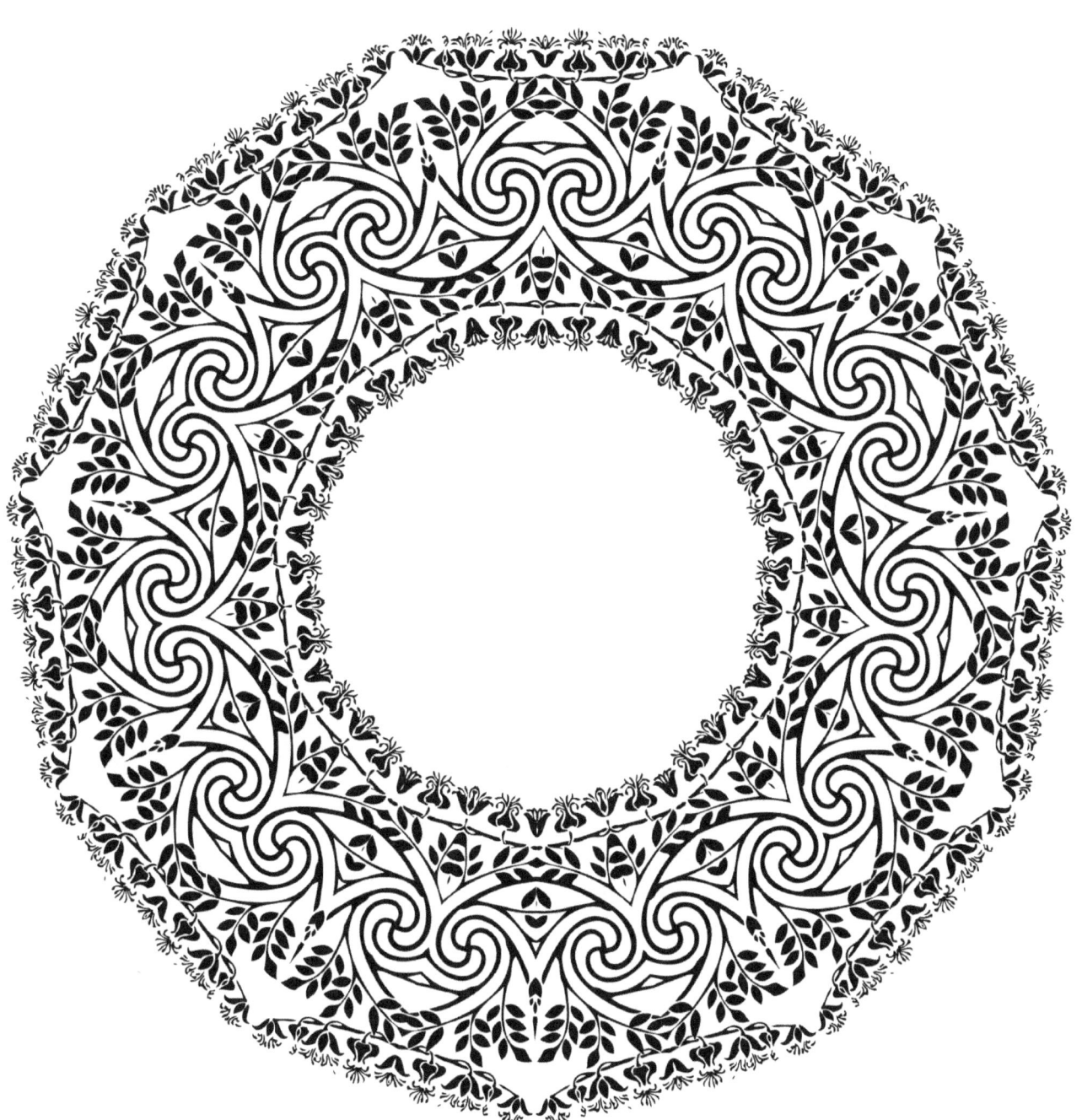

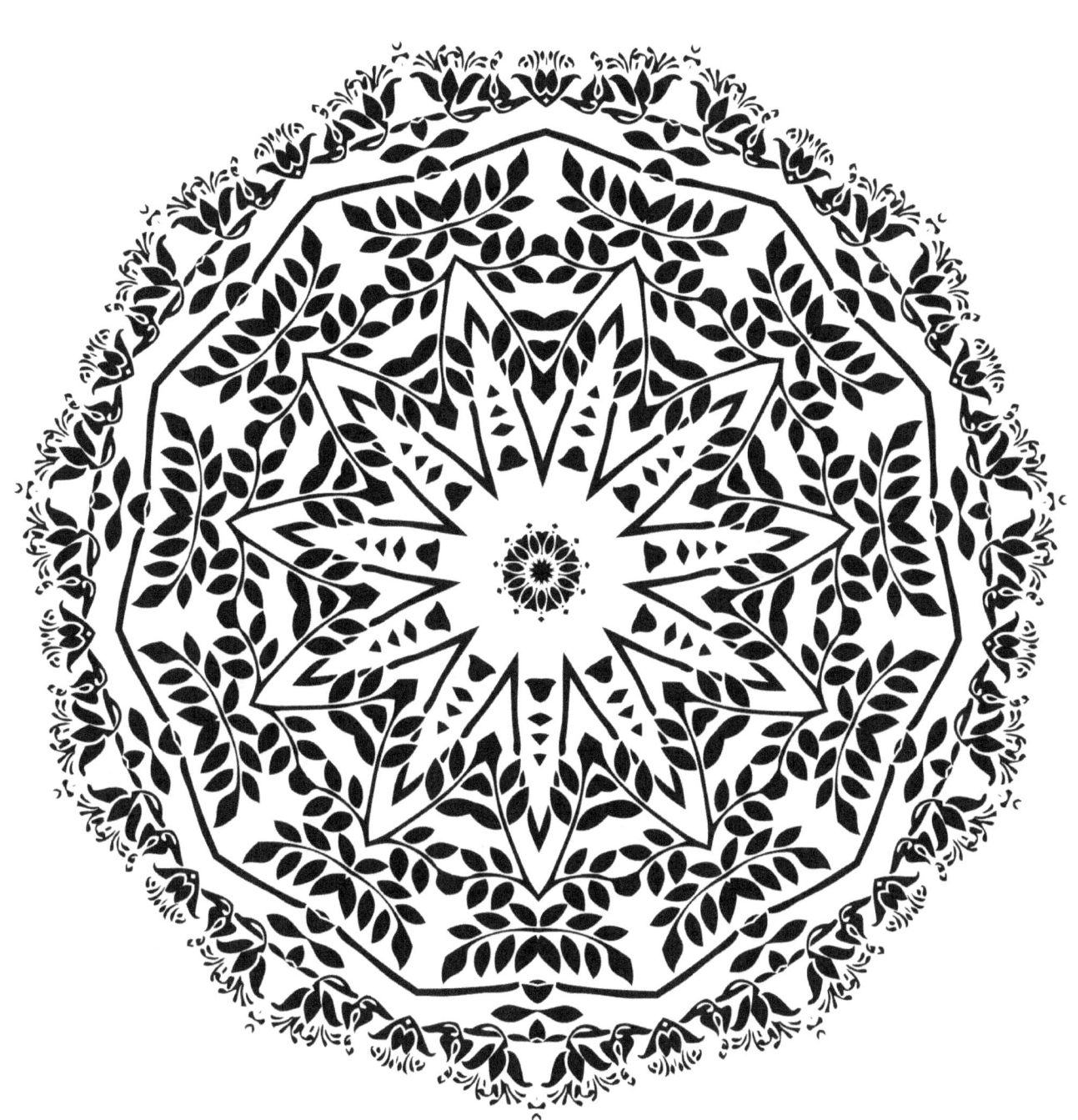

www.ingramcontent.com/pod-product-compliance
Lightning Source LLC
Chambersburg PA
CBHW081444220526
45466CB00008B/2500